THE
BIG
SHIFT

The 83 Most Important Changes That Everyone Should Know About, and the Big Shift that Changes Everything

Langdon Morris

The Big Shift:
The 83 Most Important Changes
That Everyone Should Know About,
and the
Big Shift that Changes Everything

Langdon Morris

ISBN: 978-1720470595

FutureLab Press
www.futurelabconsulting.com

ABOUT THIS BOOK

This book tells the story of our changing world, and explores what change means for our future. It's organized as an exploration of the 83 most significant changes, or shifts, that are now occurring worldwide.

But of course the individual shifts aren't nearly as significant as the fact that they're all occurring at the same time. While each one may be disruptive, 83 of them occurring all at once causes massive and unavoidable upheaval. In case you haven't noticed, it's chaos out there.

And actually it's more than upheaval and chaos, it's the complete transformation of the economy, society, and of our lives.

If this was a crime novel I'd write about a vicious criminal and an innocent victim, and in fact we have both. But since my purpose is not to entertain you with suspense I can reveal the name of killer right here on the very first page: the industrial economy is causing all this mayhem. Interestingly, the sweet and unsuspecting victim is also the industrial economy, because industrialism, through its own natural process of growth and development, has become so overwhelmingly powerful that it's become a victim of its own successes. Thus, we're in the early stages of the Big Shift from the industrial economic system we know quite well, to a very different one that we don't understand much at all.

Like a murder mystery, this story meanders its way along a series of clues, because that's really what all 83 shifts are, clues about the larger process of change and the future it may bring. I've been collecting, studying, and documenting them for 40 years and in 15 previous books (and you'll find a big pile of references starting on page 190). My purpose is to show how the clues fit together to compose a compelling story, one that helps you understand what comes next, and how to survive and thrive amid the chaos of this transformation.

ORGANIZATION OF THE BOOK

- Part 1 explores **WORLD SHIFT**, the many ways that the world is changing, and the implications of these changes for the future: **What in the world is going on?**

- Part 2 examines how and why the changing world requires of us a **MINDSET SHIFT** to understand what's happening and cope with the new demands: **How do we make sense of it?**

- Part 3 explores the **SKILL SHIFT**, new ways of strategizing, leading, organizing, and innovating that enable us to survive and thrive: **What to do about it?**

CONTENTS

PART 1:
WORLD SHIFT

PART 2:
MINDSET SHIFT

FORMAT
   Most of the shifts chronicled here are presented on two facing pages.

REFERENCES
   A selection of about 200 reference works are included beginning on page 190, organized according to the major sections of the book.

CONTENTS

PART 1

WORLD SHIFT

The End of the Industrial Economy

The way we live in today's developed world is a very recent invention. It's a product of industrial economics, which arrived around 1800 and has dominated economic and social life ever since.

Pretty much everything was different before 1800, which means that two hundred years ago society went through the process we're going through now, but of course back then it was the transition from agriculture to industry. Now it's industrialism's turn to exit the stage, as the key forces and factors that shaped the industrial era are currently undergoing fundamental and permanent change, as we will discover on the following pages.

Our challenge, however, is not only that so much change occurring. We've been living with change since 1800, as that's a central quality of industrialism too, constant innovation leading to new patterns, risks, and opportunities.

What's different now is that it's occurring faster and faster and everywhere at once, and the underlying structures are changing at the same time. We hardly have time to figure out what just happened when something else just as big or bigger hits us. This is often psychologically disturbing and it's certainly massively disruptive.

And all the changes converge to a single conclusion: industrialism is expiring, but only because of its own overwhelming success.

Consequently, when you step back and look at the pattern of change as we will do here, it's entirely evident that even the near term future will find us living in a quite different world, in the world that comes *after* industrialism.

This means that we've already entered the Big Shift, the transition era during which massive tumult, risk, and opportunity coexist, and which stretches across the full scope of human culture and thus the entirety of human civilization. With all that in mind, the focus here in Part 1 is to examine what's happening, how, and why it matters so much.

WORLD SHIFT

STRUCTURE ▶ **1**

STRUCTURE SHIFT
Basically, Everything Is Changing

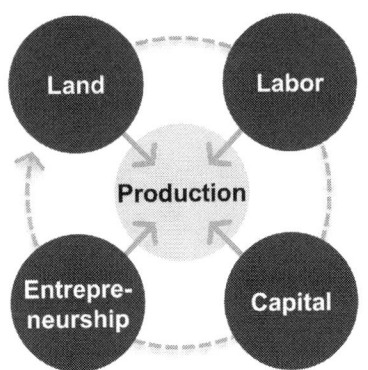

The four factors of production as defined by classical economics.

Classical economics explains that the production of value occurs as a result of the interaction of four fundamental factors: *Land*, including resources, *Labor*, people or the work force, *Capital*, money and machines, and *Entrepreneurship*, the dynamic force of innovation. As all four are now going through fundamental shifts, it's clear that within five or ten years everything will be so much different that we'll look back and realize that we've entered a new and different kind of economy. Industrialism will have come to an end, and the digital economy will have taken its place.

It makes sense to think of this as a process of structural change, meaning that it's irreversible change to the basic elements and relationships of the economic system. If you doubt this, consider the graphs on the facing page. They show that industrial employment presently constitutes only about 25 percent of the global work force and less than 20 percent in the developed world. The vast majority of work is done in services, a broad catch-all term that includes the highest paid engineers and managers along with the maids, drivers, and clerks who work for minimum wage.

How, then, can we think of ourselves as living in an industrial economy when industrial activity constitutes such a small portion of our overall effort? Indeed, with any credibility, we can't. It's definitely not where the majority of the value is being created today, nor will it be tomorrow. So naturally we ask why this is happening, and we wonder where the future *is* being created.

Technology is obviously a big part of the answer. We experience how rapidly technology is advancing, and it's impossible to ignore just how massively disruptive it is. New companies are created to exploit new technologies, and new patterns of employment emerge along with major changes in lifestyles and values.

And now we're starting to worry about all those robots and the mass unemployment they may cause, since they could have huge impact on both industrial work and services employment. What if millions of us lose our jobs?

But it's not just technology. Demographics, family patterns, education, and ways of doing business are all changing, along with other significant shifts that are also occurring throughout the natural world. These include climate change, resource shortages, deforestation and the creation of new deserts, water shortages, and mass extinctions, and together they all foretell major changes in the resource base upon which, of course, all life and thus all of civilization depends.

The combined impact of all of this will be the fundamental transformation of human society, inescapable structural change to the economy, and to everything else as well.

It will likely be messy, disruptive, and frightening, and for many of us it already is.

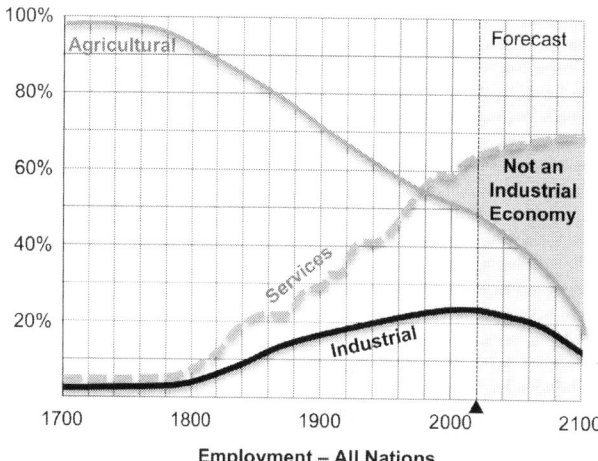

Employment – All Nations

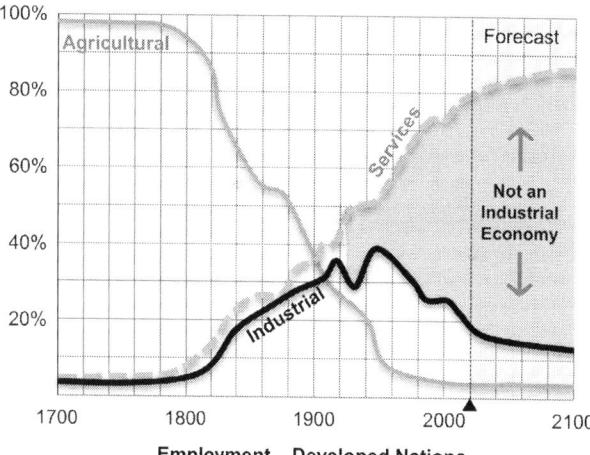

Employment – Developed Nations

2

NEXT ECONOMY SHIFT
From Industrial to ... Something Else

STRUCTURE Across the entirety of human history, tens of thousands of years of learning and development, conflict and discovery, a fundamental change in the structure of the economy such as we're experiencing today has occurred only three times previously. The control of fire occurred in the deep mists of prehistory, which enabled transformative changes in how humans lived. Much later came the development of agriculture, about 10,000 years ago, and quite recently, only two hundred years ago, arrived industrialism.

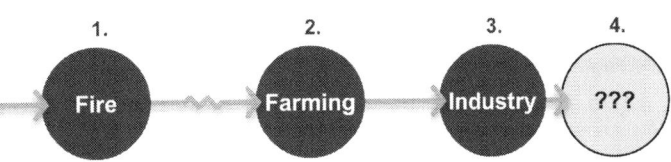

History's Four Fundamental Structural Shifts

That's it. Just three major economic transitions have occurred across all the millennia of human history. Until, now, because now we're making the fourth.

While we cannot say much about the discovery of fire, the second transition to agriculture led to the first great empires that arose at about the same time in Asia, Africa, the Americas and Europe.

Expanding populations led to the development of cities and trade, and then through the aggregation of knowledge to science and technology, which is seen in great cultural landmarks and the histories of art and architecture, statecraft and war, craft, commerce and trade. Historians describe the great ages of human history, Classical and Medieval, the Chinese Warring States and Indian Mughals, the Renaissance and the Enlightenment, all living within an economic framework defined by agriculture.

And then, Boom! Around 1800, everything changed with the invention of large scale industrialization. The entire economic process and thus the social process of human culture was transformed, abruptly organizing itself around machines and high volume production instead of plows and seeds and harvests, all of this constituting a dramatic rupture with the past.

By about 1900 after only one speedy quick century of industrialism, life for much of humanity was utterly different than it had been for the preceding thousands of years. An entirely new way of living had been created, as the explosion of industrial methods and tools led to an unimaginable abundance of food and goods that spurred a massive population explosion.

It had taken thousands of years for the human population to reach one billion, but it took only 100 more to double to two billion by about 1900, and then another 100 years to reach 7.5 billion by 2010. On the graph you see the startling vertical line showing the population explosion, clearly something entirely new in all of human history. (We will consider this in more detail in Sections 13 – 16 below.)

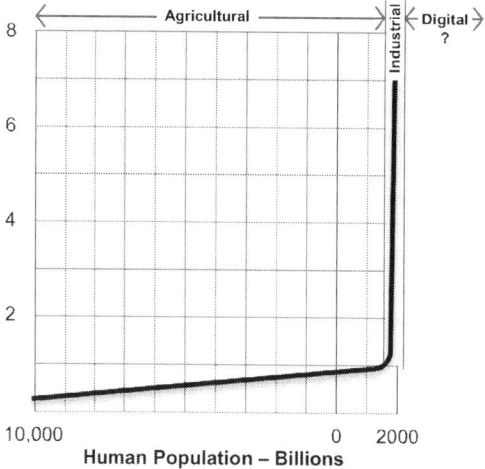

So what's next? During the next ten to twenty years, probably by 2035, the industrial economy will transition to something very different. But will it be the 'robotic economy' or the 'automation economy' dominated by robots, or the 'information economy' of databases and AI, or the 'alienation economy' characterized by social malaise and despair, or the 'climate economy' because the destruction caused by climate change will define our existence?

Perhaps it will be the 'transcendence economy' because we'll shift inwardly to focus on spiritual attainment, and it's also entirely possible that the next economy will be the 'creative economy' an era defined by human creativity in the service of higher aspirations. Throughout this book I refer to it as the 'digital economy,' obviously because of the central role that digital technology will play in organizing business, society, and life in the coming years and decades. As we proceed here I will add more details to further explain why I think so.

But in fact we cannot know exactly what's coming, nor can we know for certain what the outcomes will be. Still, there's a lot that we can foresee, so next we will explore to the central structures of the economy to discover what we can learn about change, and about the future.

3

INDUSTRIAL ECONOMICS
The Four Factors of Production

STRUCTURE

How do you even begin to think about the idea that the entire economy is going through a process of fundamental, structural change? So much is happening in so many areas that we need to find a way to organize our experiences and filter them into something useful.

As I noted above, my approach is to use the framework of classical economics. Regrettably this presents the world very simply and only in material terms, because there are only, this model tells us, the four factors of production and then the various ways of consumption. This is obviously a highly condensed version of reality that conveniently leaves aside important considerations including values, ethics, empathy, and a whole range of essentially human characteristics, not the least of which are faith and love. The intent, instead, is to describe materialism, and materialism only.

Nevertheless, if the model can explain what's happening to materialism in a useful way, and thus to help us discover why industrialism is being transformed into something else, then it's worthwhile. And while the model definitely has its limits, it does indeed enable us to discover many useful insights.

Reasoning within this economics framework, then, we know that if there is to be a major change in the structure of the economy it can come about only because some or all of the four factors of production, land, labor, capital and entrepreneurism, must change in some fundamental way. In fact, as we will shortly discover, all four are changing in fundamental ways, and the inevitable result is indeed transformative change that we are already experiencing in the tumult and chaos that surrounds us.

Below is a short paragraph describing each of the four, and on the following pages we'll look at each of them in more detail.

- The term *land* is the economist's simplified way of referring to the Earth's natural resource wealth and its climate. Both, of course, are undergoing rapid change, as resource shortages are becoming common and the impacts of climate change are getting worse.

- The term *labor* refers to us, the working people who play three essential roles in economic life: we produce, we consume, and we pay taxes. Among the relevant labor factors are the work we do, the size of the population, the rate of urbanization, and now the development and spreading use of robots. All are fundamental to the economic process, and all are also undergoing fundamental change.

- *Capital* consists of machines and money. The essence of industrialism has been the continuing replacement of people with machines, the refinement of machines and their increasing capacity to do useful work from the earliest plows and steam engines to the latest robots and Space X rockets, thus enabling the explosive growth of wealth through the operation of the industrial economic process itself. As we will examine in the sections that follow, both the machines and the money are, as with the others, experiencing fundamental changes.

- *Entrepreneurism* is the process of innovation by creating new business and social ventures that integrate land, labor, and capital into productive enterprises. The ways in which these new ventures are being created and financed are also undergoing rapid change.

What's left off our inventory of change? Basically, nothing.

Hence, the obvious point to grasp is that if *all* the factors are changing, and therefore *all* of their relationships are changing, it's thus *inevitable* that the entire economy is undergoing fundamental change. Which is exactly why it's the Big Shift.

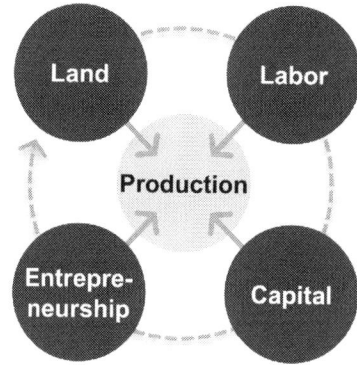

The four factors of production as defined by classical economics.

The Big Shift is the fundamental transformation of the economy from industrialism to something else.

But what?

That's the question that this book is intended to answer.

LAND

4

LAND SHIFT
From Abundance to Scarcity

'Land' as defined in economics encompasses the Earth's natural resource wealth in all its many forms, including the soil itself and water on the surface, minerals and oil below it, and forests, farms, and air on and above the surface. Today, provocatively, this also includes the climate.

We know that our natural resources are not unlimited and that we are presently consuming more than Earth produces each year, which is possible only because we are also consuming stocks of resources that nature has been storing for years, decades, and eons. As we deplete these reserves we will inevitably change our patterns of resource usage.

Further, as we consume to excess, we also produce too much waste. A key element of that waste is the CO_2 that we've released into the atmosphere, and which is warming the Earth on a gradual but significant basis. Climate change by itself poses a fundamental challenge to the future of economic activity, a challenge that will inevitably demand structural change in the economy.

Since all industrial activity requires energy, and the fossil fuels coal, oil, and gas provide the vast majority of that energy, the pace at which society will transition away from fossil fuels isn't very fast. Nevertheless, the likelihood that we will make this transition is very high, and thus the shift away from those energy sources marks yet another major change in the structure of the economy.

Given that resource shortages are already occurring, it's logical to anticipate that the industrial model of high throughput mass production will have to change significantly to address the material needs of the currently underserved billions. We have to change how we make things and how we protect the environment while doing so, or else we'll run out of clean water, clean air, trees, and countless other resources.

One essential statistic is sufficient to make the point: Economists calculate that industrial society presently consumes forty percent more natural resources than Earth produces each year. This is only possible, of course, because of nature's enormous storehouse of essential materials which industry has been tapping at a furious rate for the last 200 years.

For example, huge underground basins of oil and gas that took eons to accumulate are being drawn down in a matter of decades to power industrial society. Enormous forests that grew for thousands of years fall under the chain saw in a matter of months, huge underground aquifers that collected water for millennia are tapped out in a matter of decades, ancient seas sucked dry.

Since we don't have 1.4 Earths, we have but one, the disparity between the resources that Earth creates and our rate of consumption is obviously not sustainable. From this it's clear that the method of industrialization as considered from the perspective of 'land' is approaching its own logical conclusion as the reality of impending scarcity takes hold.

It's certainly true that innovativeness can bring resource production and consumption into balance, and indeed this is exactly what's going to happen. Accomplishing that, however, will cause the basic system to change to such an extent that the outcome will be transformative – the economic system is going to change fundamentally simply because resources and climate will not permit anything else.

The Aral Sea was once the fourth largest in the world, covering 26,000 square miles. But in the 1960s the rivers feeding the sea were diverted for agriculture, and it has shrunk to become only some small lakes. Now it's known as the Aralkum Desert.

In China, the 2013 National Water Census revealed that 28,000 Chinese rivers had gone missing, dried up due to overuse.

Ma Jun, a Chinese water expert at the Institute of Public and Environmental Affairs in Beijing explains, 'One of the major reasons is the over-exploitation of the underground water reserves, while environmental destruction is another reason, because desertification of forests has caused a rain shortage in the mountain areas.' (Katy Yan, International Rivers)

Poyang was once China's largest freshwater lake, averaging 1400 square miles in surface area. By 2012 it had shrunk to 77 square miles due to overuse and the upstream damming of the Yangtze River.

5

FARM SHIFT
From High Labor to High Technology

LAND

For a mere $500,000 the John Deere company would be very happy to sell you a brand new combine tractor with which to harvest your massive Nebraska corn crop. Equipped with a GPS device accurate to within one inch (2.5 cm), it will steer itself along in perfectly straight rows. In the cab of the harvester you'll view seven digital screens, each displaying a different type of information among the 22 that the combine is collecting, all with the intent to help you become a more efficient farmer.

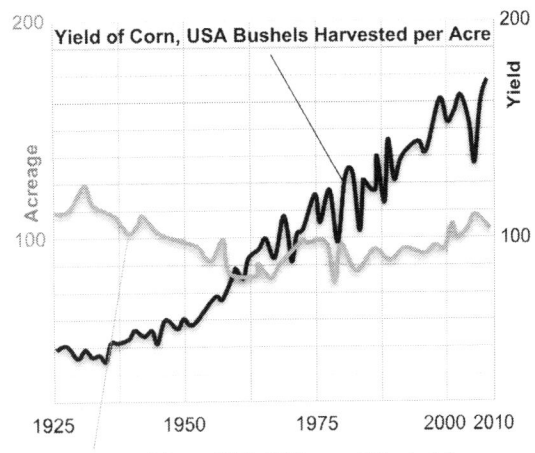

From this we can easily see that corn farming in the US Midwest has become a digital profession, now known as 'agri-tech' or 'precision agriculture.' The result shows in the graph as a boom in the productivity of corn farms in the US, a three-fold improvement in productivity yield over the last century.

What the graph doesn't show is the drastic decline in the number of people needed. In fact, today there are far more cows than people in Nebraska, as the number of farmers needed to tend the state's 10 million acres of corn fields has been declining while productive yields have been increasing. Today three people can effectively manage a vast corn production as large as 2000 acres.

1200 miles to the west in California's strawberry fields, the nasty lygus bug turns lovely red fruits into misshapen lumps, and to remove them farmers use a giant 'bug vacuum,' a clever form of pest removal that reduces the need for chemicals. In nearby strawberry-growing greenhouses, meanwhile, instead of soil the growing medium is ground coconut husks that doesn't require fumigants, while water consumption is about one-tenth of the amount needed for growing the crop in the ground. Further south in California, lettuce grown in a giant greenhouse is protected from bugs by garlic sprayed by a robot that roams the aisles, taking care of the job that humans once considered the most unpleasant task in the greenhouse.

All this reminds us of what Daniel Webster noted a century ago, that 'When tillage begins other arts follow. The farmers therefore are the founders of human civilization.' This accurately describes how industrialism got its start as an offshoot of farming, and still describes how many innovations find their way into cities. Self-driving vehicles, robots, water conservation, reduced chemical usage, drones, these and many more are being pioneered on farms.

The digitalization of farming, whether you call it precision agriculture or agri-tech or robo-farming, involves satellite technology and digital market-making, software analysis and robotic workers, plant genetics, and alternatives to pesticides, and it's a global phenomenon that has impacts throughout the entire farming cycle, from selecting crops to grow, planting, growing and harvesting, bringing to market, and caring for the land.

Far away from the massive corn farms of the Midwestern USA, farmers in Zambia in Southern Africa generate about 20 percent of the country's overall economic production, about $4 billion, while employing 75 percent of the country's 17 million people. The Zambia Agricultural Research Institute also uses advanced technology, applying genetic engineering to cultivate new plant variations. It also encourages farmers to plant a wider variety of crops to help diversify local diets and improve nutrition and health, and its method is to issue electronic vouchers that farmers can use to buy seeds and supplies. Yes, technology is infiltrating everywhere.

Industrial agriculture mechanized the manual process, while digital agriculture is the application of even more advanced technologies to make farming even more productive – digital machines, digital genetics, digital soil and water management, digital vouchers, satellites, etc., etc. It's still farming, but as we see, even the life of the soil is transformed by the power of technology. It will also be transformed, but in a bad way, by the acceleration of climate change.

In the words of strawberry farmer Steven Newell, 'We're almost more of a technology company than a farm or produce company.'

Adds Nebraska corn farmer Scott Wagner, 'We are better environmentalists because of technology.'

Hana Medina
Costco Connection
April 2018

6

CLIMATE SHIFT
From Temperate to Volatile

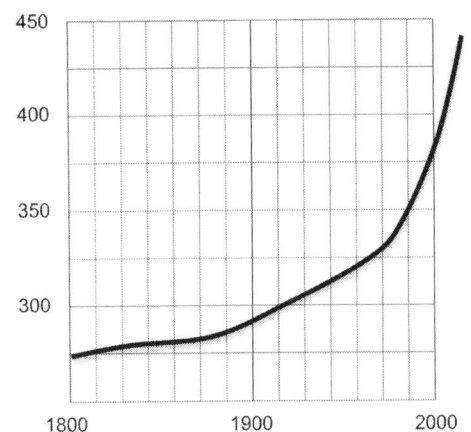

CO2 Concentration in the Atmosphere - Parts per Million

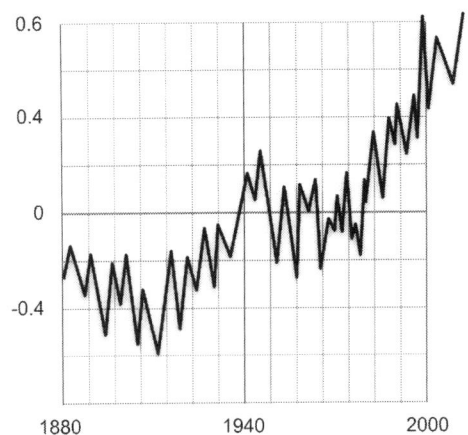

Global Surface Temperature Anomaly (°C)

LAND

During the 20th century the global climate was more benign than during any century in two millennia, and this helped enormously as we built the industrial economy. Now the bill is coming due, however, as all that CO2 we created by burning fossil fuels is changing the climate, and benign is no the longer the right description. Under all but the most moderate of possible outcomes, the social and economic impact of climate change will be transformative.

Even moderate outcomes will cause extensive social, cultural, and personal tragedies, as homes, fortunes, and lives will disappear into more violent storms and beneath rising oceans. Low-lying nations such as Vanuatu and the Maldives are likely to disappear entirely, and low-lying coastal cities will see luxury high rise towers will be peeking up through crashing waves, submerged and accessible only by boats.

Disruptions to food supplies will create chaos and crisis, and mass migrations will likely arise at an unprecedented scale, creating gigantic cities of millions of refugees with slim prospects for a better life.

Bad and worst-case outcomes include coastal flooding that will render trillions of dollars of today's most highly valued real estate completely worthless. Will the owners keep paying their huge mortgages after their property has become submerged and worthless? The stress on the financial sector will be enormous, progressively worsening as defaults mount. Will insurers be able to pay the massive claims, or will they collapse under the weight of unmanageable losses? The shift has begun already, as some property insurers now refuse to provide coverage for coastal properties.

When the lending and insurance sectors come under such extreme stress then intense pressure will come to bear on governments to bail everyone out. The wealthy will relocate, but still insist on compensation for their lost multi-million dollar beach condos, although they'll probably be less demanding about compensation for modest coastal homes and shacks.

The poor will also suffer; indeed, the deep impacts of climate change are going to fall most heavily on the poor and poorest since they lack the resources to relocate to safer and higher ground. They'll be the ones flooded out of coastal homes without recourse and without the resources to relocate, they are the ones most likely to be trapped in the newly created, climate change induced deserts. This will cause economic and social disparities between rich and poor to widen, accentuating the moral and ethical dimensions along with the weather, water, food, and housing impacts.

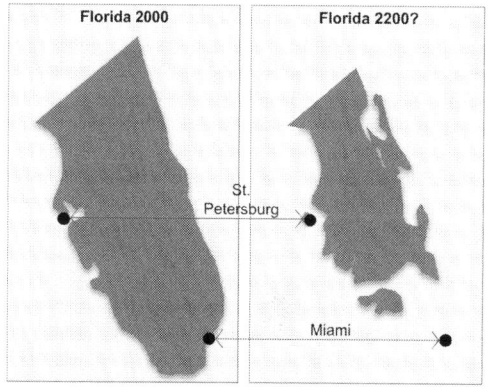

The lost assets will not only be residences. When Wall Street floods and its towers become unusable, when the same occurs in Shanghai, London, and Mumbai, what then? First, second and third order impacts compound upon one another, the tragedy spreads, and the financial burdens multiply. A drastic phase of economic contraction could easily result.

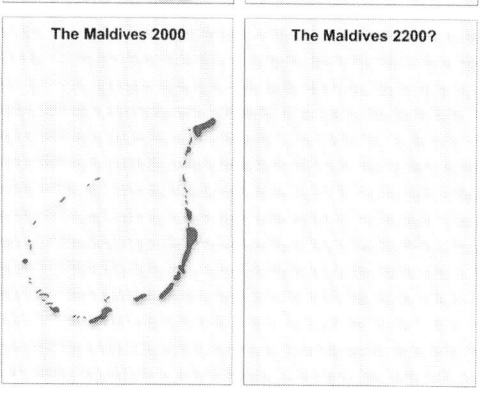

Of course this story will likely unfold over decades, which will allow time for adjustment, although it could come much faster, depending on how fast the ice sheets melt. Ports can be rebuilt, and houses, factories, and offices too. But the infrastructure that the economy operates upon has taken a century and many trillions of dollars to build, and it cannot be replaced even over decades without major financial and social stress. Hence, what we see is that industrialization itself created climate change, and now climate change will invoke fundamental change throughout industry. The challenges faced by the global energy industry will be among the most difficult to manage.

7

ENERGY SHIFT
From Old Fossils to New Sun

LAND

Energy has been society's defining resource throughout the history of civilization. When our ancestors discovered how to use fire for heat, light, and cooking it undoubtedly transformed the very structure of life. Anthropologists suggest that the adoption of cooking enabled fundamental changes in human physiology that led to the development of a much larger brain, possibly the trigger that led to the evolution of modern *homo sapiens*.

About ten thousand years ago those larger-brained humans learned to capture the sun's energy as trapped by plants, and so created agriculture. Then, around 1800, we learned to use the sun's energy that had been trapped millions of years ago as fossil fuels, and since then fossil fuels have been the indispensable enabler of industrialization, as the graph to the left shows. There would be no industrial economy and thus no modern or post-modern society without fossil fuels, burned in massive quantities to power factories and cars, homes and offices, computers and TVs and everything else.

But nor would there be climate change. And the climate change question causes us inevitably to consider our energy sources, for as we are confronted with severe climate change impacts, then the nations of world will be obliged by prudence and by public pressure to bring a halt to the use of fossil fuels. Thus, if we frame the issue as 'fossil fuels vs civilization,' as we eventually will, then the oil, gas, and coal industries will inevitably have to be legislated out of existence.

This transition has already begun. The term 'energy-transition risk' is now used in the investment sector to describe to financial exposure due to the anticipated contraction of the fossil fuel industry.

While the transition to non-fossil sources has been going on for decades and significant progress has been made to improve the cost effectiveness of solar and wind generation and mass scale battery storage (see

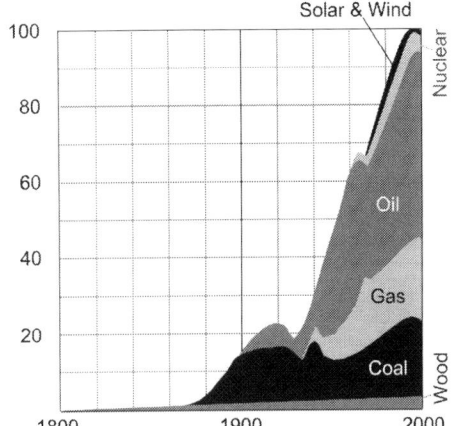

Total US Energy Use – Quads
After Vaclav Smil
Global Catastrophes and Trends

the graph to the right), oil, gas, and coal still provide the predominant share of all the world's energy. As the graph on the facing page shows, in 2000 fossil fuels provided more than 90% of our energy, and oil companies remain among the world's largest and most valuable.

But suppose that one day, perhaps in a decade or two, the oil companies are legislated out of business and made to disappear, stranding their remaining assets in the ground. All their shareholder equity would abruptly turn to dust, a traumatic burden for the markets (and remember that they'll already be stressed due to the financial burdens of coastal flooding).

This would also be disastrous for oil producing nations that rely on oil for their national incomes, such as Russia, Nigeria, Angola, Venezuela, and Saudi Arabia. Remove oil-related income and they instantly enter economic crises, with massive social unrest sure to follow.

Would the Russians, who currently do not cooperate well with other nations, even go along with a shutdown of their oil industries? Would the Saudis? Would Europeans be willing to trigger riots across Nigeria when its oil industry shuts down? Would they invest billions of Euros to prop up the Nigerian economy to compensate for the lost income? Or in the Angolan?

How, then, are we going to handle these conflicts? Will we favor the interests of oil producing companies and nations over those of nations that will be most severely damaged or entirely flooded out by extreme climate change? Or vice versa? We will surely face very difficult questions for which there are no easy answers.

•••

That, then, is the perspective we gain by considering the Land and its major elements, natural resources, farming, climate, and energy. All have reached inherent limits, and so inevitably all are being transformed beyond the logic of industrialism into something quite different. Let us now turn to Labor.

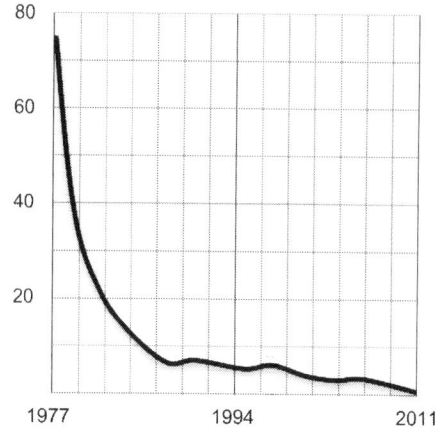

Price of crystalline silicon photovoltaic cells – $ / watt

'According to the International Energy Agency, the Chinese public and private sectors will invest more than $6 trillion in low-carbon power generation and other clean technologies by 2040.

The Chinese renewable energy sector already boasts 125 gigawatts of installed solar power, over twice the amounts in the US and Germany. Chinese firms now have the capacity to manufacture 51 gigawatts worth of photovoltaic solar panels every year.'

Amy Myers Jaffe
Foreign Affairs
March/April 2018

LABOR  **8**

LABOR SHIFT
From People to Robots

At the beginning of the industrial era around 1800, the entire workforce consisted of animal and people power, supplemented with a bit of fire, wind and water. People were the builders and the diggers, the makers, the drivers, managers, and the clerks who built the companies that built industry.

Everyone worked, from young children through middle age and even the aged, for there was no such thing as public education or retirement then: the choice was to work or suffer from unemployment and its poverty.

More people came to work in factories as industry expanded. Their children did as well, and generations of laborers provided the raw effort and intelligence that created economic growth.

By the early 1900s, industrialism was booming, with thriving industries in steel, autos, energy, clothing, food, housewares, and chemicals, among many others. By the middle of the century low cost autos and a boom in highway construction enabled suburbia to erupt across the landscape on a mass scale. Factories and the pollution they produced were gradually relocated away from the cities, but still the basic pattern of high volume production to enable high volume consumption continued to drive the economy forward. People kept the production lines moving.

Today, however, as the nature of production changes and becomes more automated, the demand for industrial workers is declining. Robots in vast numbers are already performing massive amounts of work, and their numbers will only grow during the next decade and beyond. Exactly how far this wave of automation will go no one knows, and thus we are unsure how much human labor will be displaced by digital labor. But the possibility that extensive substitution of robots for people will lead to a rapid decline in the need for humans is inescapable and frightening.

Consider what would happen if robots replaced ten percent of the workers in developed nations, and they weren't able to find other employment (not everyone can become a computer programmer, after all). A ten percent jump in unemployment is the prescription for a severe recession. But suppose that twenty or thirty percent of the human workforce was not longer needed? What then?

That's the scenario for a global depression, shown to the right below as Scenario 2, a massive labor market contraction throughout the economy that would induce a brutal downward spiral of deflation. Will it come to that? Again, no one knows. What we do know is that more robots are being used each year, and some forecasts suggest that within a few years, perhaps around 2023 or 2024, we'll be using as many as 100 billion of them. That's more than twenty robots for each worker.

Is that an industrial economy in the way that we understand industrialism today? Absolutely not.

Robots exist at all, of course, and they are able function at such a high level of proficiency, because of highly advanced technology, particularly computer chips and the massively complex code they run. Chips are now everywhere, from that annoying ten cent device inside the throwaway musical greeting card to the supreme work of engineering, the $120 processor and logic board that powers your indispensable iPhone.

To fully grasp the future prospects for labor we have to understand more about robots, and to understand them we have to take a deeper look at their key enabling technology, the computer chip.

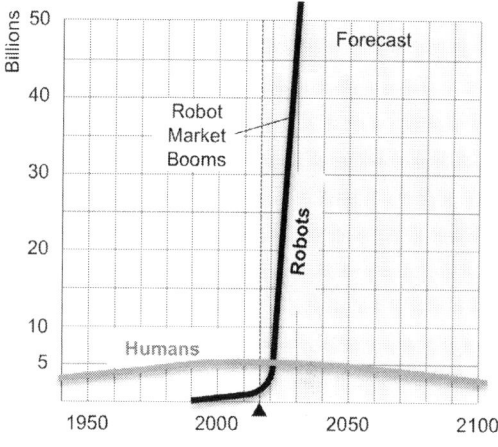

Composition of the Work Force, Scenario 1

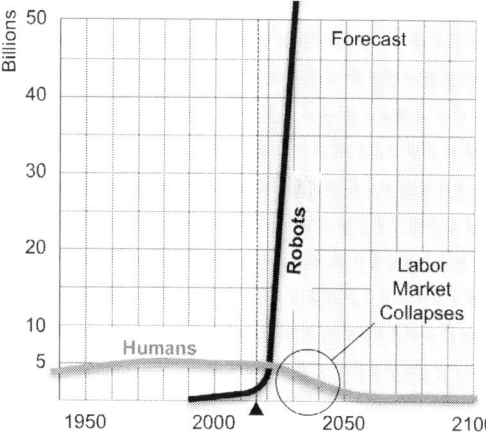

Composition of the Work Force, Scenario 2

9

COMPUTER CHIP SHIFT
From Manual to Digital

LABOR

By the 1830s metallurgy and machines had gotten so good that Charles Babbage and Ada Lovelace were able to realistically envision a 'computation engine' that would shift calculation from a manual job with a pencil to digital one by machine. Their vision was realized with the development of the ENIAC in the 1940s, and digital technology began to accelerate with the invention of transistors in the 1950s, and then computer chips came along in the 1960s and changed everything. The digital revolution was on in earnest, and now chips are everywhere, in everything, a tremendous force that's disrupting existing business patterns, geopolitics, and human relationships throughout society and the economy.

Chips get faster, more powerful, and amazingly, less expensive with each succeeding product generation, and since there is so much money to be made with the next better chip, chip makers have relentless incentive to continue their remarkable streak of progress.

Gordon Moore noticed this progress in 1965 and his observation became known as *Moore's Law*, describing the fact that computer chip capacities and speeds double about every two years even as cost declines along the reciprocal curve. This amazing rate of progress has been sustained for the last half century, and now the global economy, including farming, is entirely reliant upon chips and the digital infrastructure of the internet that enables instantaneous flow of information from anywhere to everywhere. With each technical advance the capacity of machines to make useful calculations improves significantly, thereby increasing our dependence.

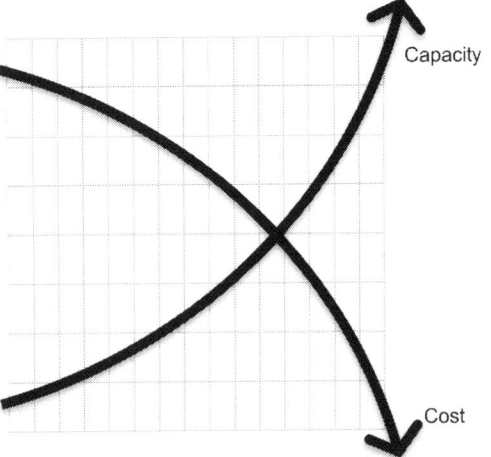

Capacity

Cost

Computer Chips: Capacity Up, Cost Down
The Capacity Curve is also know as Moore's Law.

For a glimpse at how digital technology has advanced, consider that the $500 iPhone of 2007 was about 1000 times *more* powerful than the $9 million Cray computer of 1977. Please take a moment to reread that stunning sentence. It's an impressive *18 million-fold* improvement. Yikes!

Highly capable robots are soon to be a major part of the story, and if robots fulfill even a modest portion of their potential then the next phases of digitalization will be, as noted above, even more impactful and thus more disruptive, possibly wiping out millions of jobs.

Industry forecasts project that the total number of chips in use will increase roughly by a factor of 10 during the coming few years, spreading technology further across all phases of commerce, culture, and life. As these chips will become better every year, both more powerful and cheaper, they'll take over still more and more functions. Which functions? Health care is shifting to be digital, finance is already entirely digital, entertainment, information, news, advertising, communications, publishing, buying and selling, nearly all are fully digitized now, all enabled by computer chips. Consequently, today the world's biggest ad agency isn't an ad agency, it's Google (see box to the right); the biggest retailers aren't just traditional retailers, the list includes Amazon.com and Alibaba; and the most significant phone maker used to be a computer company, Apple.

Industrialism remains at the heart of this because industry enabled the scientific and technological advances that make it possible for computer chips to impact all facets of economic activity. Thus, industry created computer chips and now computer chips are transforming industry.

Looking ahead, the combined impact of all the new digital capabilities will inevitably result in the continuing transformation of the economy, and the replacement of industrialism with its sequel. There will still be industrial activities, of course, and we'll still depend on them. But as they're becoming ever more automated and require less and less human involvement, the way we think about, manage, and act in the economy is already changing. It's the digital shift.

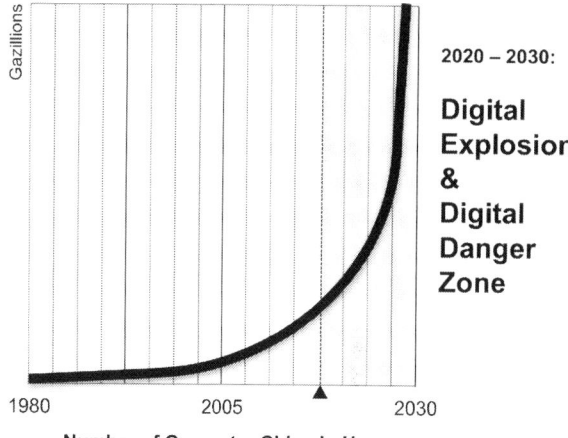

2020 – 2030:

Digital Explosion & Digital Danger Zone

Number of Computer Chips in Use

'The Pentium IIs we used in the first year of Google (1997) performed about 100 million floating point operations per second. The GPUs we use today (2017) perform about 20 trillion such operations — a factor of about 200,000 difference — and our very own TPUs (special chips for AI applications) are now capable of 180 *trillion* (180,000,000,000,000) floating point operations per second.'

Sergey Brin
Co-founder, Google
2017 Founders' Letter

10

DIGITAL SHIFT
From Invention to Saturation

LABOR Numeracy is the ability to count and calculate with numbers. It originated unknown thousands of years ago, but then about five thousand years ago with the invention and spread of money the ability to count became an essential skill and it spread quickly throughout civilization.

A computer chip is, at root, just a fancy and speedy device for counting, and as Babbage and Lovelace understood nearly 200 years ago, when you can count you can do much more than just count, you can organize, design, decide, and act. Today, as a result, even a pretty basic car has 30 to 50 computer chips that control nearly everything from acceleration to braking to gear shifting, along with all the various motors that operate windows and wipers. Chips are also essential to the many sensors that monitor the car's functioning, its position, and its surroundings. A luxury car with even more gizmos and gadgets may have 100 chips, along with as many as 100 to 200 *million* lines of computer code that tell the chips what to do.

This partly explains why hardly anyone can fix their own cars any more. Digital diagnostics are essential, and Tesla cars perform software-driven self-diagnostics continuously. When necessary, they're reprogrammed from the central factory location because they're connected wirelessly to the internet. So, too, by the way, are the jet engines your airline uses to fly you around the world, which are monitored remotely and constantly so no one has to look inside to know how the engine is performing.

What this conquest of society by the computer chip suggests is that a car is no longer a car as we have previously thought of it, it's really just a computer with wheels. A road, the one covered with sensors, is a computer for driving the other computers upon. A house is a computer for living in, an office one for working in, and clothing is computers for wearing.

Where this logic takes us is to the recognition that fairly soon we'll stop thinking about computers as separate things, because computing capabilities will be embedded everywhere. The term 'computer' will likely disappear from common usage, or else switch back to refer to a person with advanced math skills as it did half a century ago before the PC and the internet

Knowing, then, that computer chips are the small (and getting smaller), inexpensive (and getting cheaper), and quiet enablers of the digital economy that are hidden away inside of every device, and knowing that chips are continuing to get more powerful and less expensive, we also gain insight into why robots are now becoming common: the chips they require are now so powerful that they can perform the massive volume of information processing that is required for robots to become useful.

Thus, at the current rate of improvement in ten years a generic computer chip will be about thirty times more powerful than today's comparably generic chip. Imagine, then, what a magnificent metallic thinking beast you'll be able to create in a decade, and then consider what the economic impact is likely to be, and the likelihood of a digital revolution takes hold in your mind. As robots get better, human workers will become even more expendable.

The robots are coming ...

11

ROBOT SHIFT
From Fiction to Fact

LABOR

A restaurant named Spyce recently opened in Boston, notable because it operates a kitchen that is staffed almost entirely with robots, the prototype having been developed in the basement of an MIT frat house. By the time you read this Spyce may be a distant memory, but then again perhaps it will be the next McDonald's, with hundreds of locations and thousands of robots.

Robots have been living in our imaginations for centuries, laboring for us to improve our lives and remove drudgery. Greek myths described machines that moved on their own many centuries before Mary Shelly's story of Dr. Frankenstein, and it will not surprise you that Leonardo da Vinci sketched designs for a mechanical military knight that we would today think of as a robot. In our own time, these myths along with countless science fiction stories are quickly becoming science and social facts.

The first crude and very experimental robots were built in labs in the 1970s, and now as we approach their half-century robots are commonplace and highly productive laborers.

Of course we find more uses for them now that their capabilities are increasing so fast, which is a result of the increasing power of their computer chips and the increasing skill of programmers who write the necessary computer code.

How many are there? Amazon.com reportedly uses more than 50,000 warehouse robots, 25,000 more than the company used just 2 years ago. We might call them 'digital laborers,' but the idea that machines replace humans is not a new story. In fact, it is the essential story of industrialization.

The mechanization of agriculture and manufacturing during the 1800s enabled the transformation of the economy and society in every respect, so what we're experiencing is perhaps just the next steps in this process.

What all robots have in common is that they perceive their environments through arrays of sensors, process the collected data to determine patterns and decide actions, and act in their environments to produce outcomes. That is, they accomplish work.

As nearly all of this was formerly done by people, we fear that robots may displace human workers on such a large scale as to cause massive unemployment, and thus massive social disruption. When robots run the farms and the factories and drive the vehicles and cook the meals you begin to wonder if people will have any work to do at all. And yes, soon there will be sex robots (sexbots), as many companies anticipate a huge market and are already quite far along in their development.

Hence, we have to ask if they will cause mass unemployment or enable mass leisure. If we follow the economic logic of industrialism in which all factors of production are made into commodities, then unemployment is probably the outcome, but the social costs of this will be so enormous that we may indeed choose a different way. This, too, implies a different economic logic, not industrialism but something else.

Another intriguing and also intimidating prospect is that robots will eventually design, build, and then quickly improve other robots at a pace so fast that humans are left behind entirely. This scary possibility even has a name: it's called the 'singularity.'

Some of today's most useful robots are simple devices only by today's high standards. Amazon robots organize stacks of bins so humans can pick the items you ordered, small robots vacuum your carpets, security robots roam parking garages, while gigantic mining trucks go up and down the mine roads without human drivers.

'CIMON' is NASA's AI robot on the International Space Station, Baxter a delivery robot in hospitals, and countless companies and universities are working on new ones with the intention of creating new products, or just as learning tools to train the next generations of robot designers and engineers.

12

SINGULARITY SHIFT
From Simple Robots to Very Smart Ones

LABOR The terms 'artificial intelligence' and 'machine learning' describe the capacity of machines to gather information, make interpretations, and initiate actions to achieve desired outcomes, all with little or no human participation. When we peer a bit further into the future we wonder what might happen when the power of a computer approaches the processing power of a human brain. Would that computer be as 'smart' as a human? And how long would it take for that computer to design and build a family of still better computers, thereby rapidly accelerating their own development and leaving humans a distant second in brainpower, relegated to an entirely dystopian and post-human landscape?

The possibility that computers will equal and then exceed human intelligence, and then through a spiraling process of self-improvement far surpass humanity, has been given the name 'singularly.' The technical meaning of singularity, a term borrowed from physics, is the point in time and space at which the known rules break down into something quite else, quite unknown, and presently unrecognizable. A black hole is a singularity in physics, and so is the super-smart, uber-brained robot for human society.

By charting the historical development of computing power and projecting it into the future, computer scientist Ray Kurzweil has forecast that by the 2040s the computation power of chips will reach and then surpass that of humans. According to Kurzweil's calculation, computers capable of simulating human brains will exist by 2025, and by 2045 nonbiological intelligence will be one billion times *more* powerful than all human intelligence was in 2005. This is the point at which humans become evolutionarily obsolete,

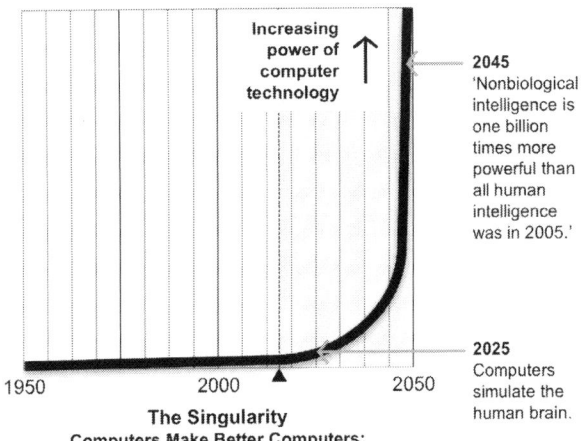

Increasing power of computer technology ↑

2045
'Nonbiological intelligence is one billion times more powerful than all human intelligence was in 2005.'

2025
Computers simulate the human brain.

1950　2000　2050

The Singularity
Computers Make Better Computers;
Are Humans Obsolete?

surpassed by our digital creations. What this will mean for the digital economy is impossible to predict, but fascinating to consider.

Kurzweil makes a strong argument in his fascinating 600 page book *The Singularity is Near*, but he could just as easily be completely wrong. Perhaps computers will never become *that* powerful; perhaps essential qualities of thought and intelligence actually cannot be replicated in computer code; perhaps the economy will falter and economic progress will stop before the singularity arrives; perhaps human-level robotic intelligence will be outlawed. But if Kurzweil is right, and his forecast does indeed come to pass, what then? Then, everything changes...

•••

Did you notice how the series of topics under discussion here has progressed? The main theme we're presently examining is supposedly 'labor,' but to consider what's happening with labor we've had to make a significant detour to discuss technology, robots, and now super-intelligence and the singularity. In economic terms computers and robots are 'capital,' not 'labor,' but they replace and displace labor at potentially such a massive scale that the line between the two blurs to nothing. This, too, is a reflection of how industrialism is evolving.

Thus, we discover the looping nature of any conversation about the future, how everything connects to everything else and how complexity balloons. There's much more to explore in the realms of capital and technology, but for the moment we'll return to labor, to the people, and take a look at what's been happening with our homes and living patterns, and think about the impact on society and population growth. After all, population growth has also been an essential part of the story of industrialization by providing the new laborers and consumers necessary for the industrial economy to grow.

As we will shortly discover, however, things are changing there as well.

'The Singularity is a future period during which the pace of technological change will be so rapid, its impact so deep, that human life will be irreversibly transformed.

Within several decades, information-based technologies will encompass all human knowledge and proficiency.

By the end of the 21st century, the nonbiological portion of our intelligence will be trillions of trillions of times more powerful than unaided human intelligence.

We are now in the early stages of this transition.'

Ray Kurzweil
The Singularity is Near

13

URBAN SHIFT
From County to City

LABOR When the industrial era began in about 1800 only about three percent of the population lived in cities and towns, but both push and pull changed all that. The mechanization of farming made huge numbers of farm workers superfluous and pushed them off the land, while the lure of the city attracted them with its entertainments and delights, the large pool of potential mates, and factory jobs.

Since then the world's cities have been growing rapidly, ballooning from 30 million (3 percent of 1 billion in 1800), to 280 million (14 percent of 2 billion in 1900), to 3.75 *billion* (50 percent of 7.5 billion) by 2010.

But while cities continue to grow as more and more people migrate into them from the countryside, the last thirty years have begun to see a surprising reversal of the population explosion. The growth rate that many feared would continue to increase has in fact started to reverse, and it's clear now that the nature of city life itself explains why.

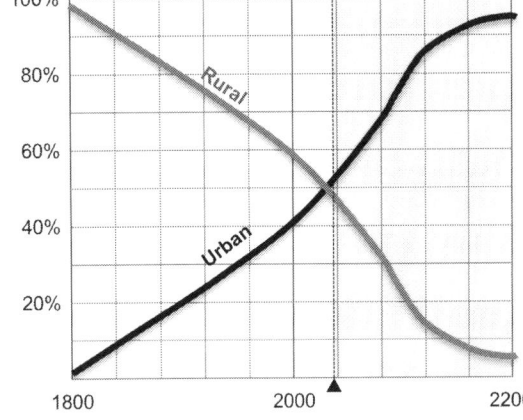

World Population, by Percent

World Population, Billions

To understand the relationship between urbanization and population it's useful to think of the family as an economic unit, and to consider the differences between rural and urban families. On a typical farm, children are valued laborers who work nearly for free. Since there's always unlimited work to do on a farm, more children means more work gets done, and since a child produces more than he or she consumes, children are economic assets for their parents. Consequently, farm families tend to be large as long as the land being worked is also proportionately large.

Factory workers living in the urban setting develop an entirely different family pattern. In cities, children are not producers but consumers, and nearly everything they require is expensive. Food, clothing, living space, and especially education, and since education is the best way upward on the economic ladder of society, parents must also invest time in their education. Living in urban settings, then, the logical economic choice for most families is to have fewer children than they would have had on the farm, often only one or two.

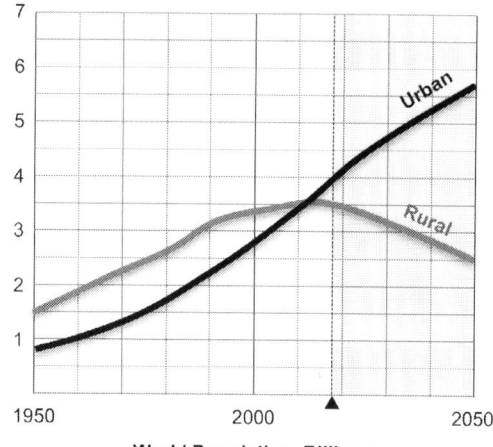

World Population, Billions

This change in the birth pattern would not have much effect on the overall rate of population growth if the majority of the population was still living in the countryside, but during the 20th century the scale of urban migration was furiously fast. With fewer people in rural settings having many children, and more living in urban settings having fewer children, the overall rate of population growth would naturally be expected to slow, and so it has.

The key to forecasting the future rate of population growth, then, is to determine the rate of urbanization. What percent of the population is expected to be living in cities in the future?

And the answer is that migration into cities is continuing, and by the midpoint of the 21st century, urban dwellers will constitute at least 75 percent of the population, and by the end of this century fully 90 to 95 percent of humanity will be urbanized.

The consequences for the rate of population growth are already evident: population growth will most likely stop entirely, and then reverse. Urbanization will thus transform the population explosion into the population *implosion*, a process with enormous implications both socially and economically. As we will shortly see, this is still more evidence that the end of industrialization is upon us.

14

DEMOGRAPHIC SHIFT
From Explosion to Implosion

LABOR

Early in the industrial era economists became alarmed at the rate of population growth, famous among them Thomas Malthus, who warned in 1798 that the population was growing exponentially but that the food supply could not grow nearly that fast. He predicted that mass starvation would be the inevitable result. His forecast was wrong, however, as food production expanded due to both mechanization and other forms of innovation, including fertilizers, pesticides, and crop genetics.

By the 1960s the population reached 5 billion, growth was still accelerating, and doom was again in the forecast. Paul Ehrlich's provocatively titled book *The Population Bomb* projected mass starvation as the human population would approach and then pass ten billion.

But again the bomb did not explode. In fact something quite different happened, when, as we saw above, the unexpected family dynamics of urbanization altered the pattern. And now that two centuries of migration to the cities has fundamentally altered reproduction rates, the population boom is becoming an implosion.

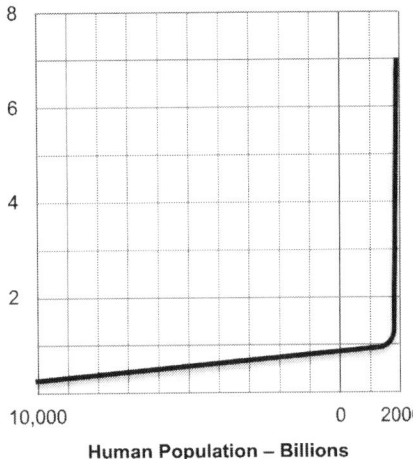

Human Population – Billions

The shape of the population curve from antiquity until today, in the figure to the left, shows slow but steady population growth from 10,000 BC until the dawn of industrialism, and then a booming population for the following two hundred years represented by the nearly vertical, quite scary line.

But then the affect of urbanization kicks in, and between today and 2150 the boom abruptly ends as the population fully urbanizes and the birthrate drops, as shown on the facing page.

Does that surprise you? It surprises nearly everyone, as the mental model we carry around says nothing about the end of the explosion. But that is in fact what's happening.

Thus, if we take the shape of the population curve as a description of human economic history, we see three very distinct phases, as shown to the right and below:

- Phase 1 is *Agricultural*, slow and steady population increase.
- Phase 2 is *Industrial*, a population boom with the line streaking nearly vertically.
- Phase 3 is whatever comes next (I have suggested Digital), during which we see gradual population decline.

The economic question this raises is, 'Can an economic model created during Phase 2's population boom sustain itself under Phase 3's steady decline?'

It appears that the answer is, 'No, it cannot.'

Even considering the amazing inventiveness of today's entrepreneurs and indeed of people across the entire economy, it hardly seems plausible that industrialism will continue in its present form. Thus, just as industrialism was fundamentally different from agriculture, the likelihood that what follows industrialism won't be much like industrialism is also very high.

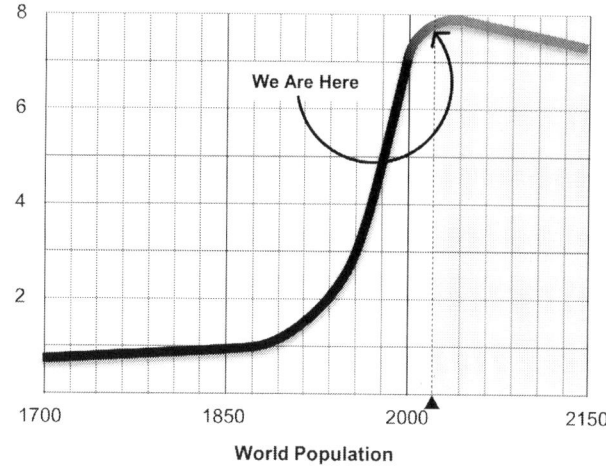

World Population

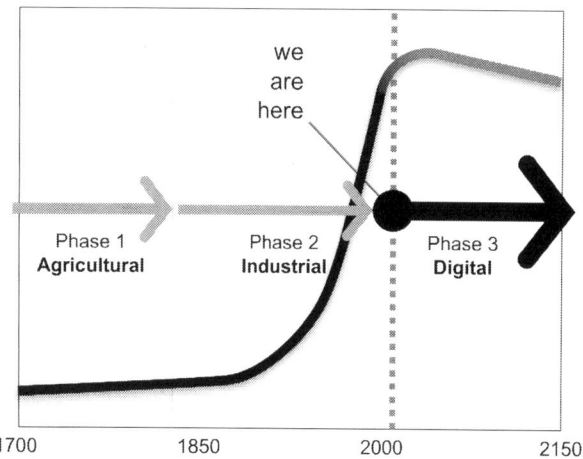

One of the most basic reasons for this is that while young people consume goods in abundance, as they age they tend to consume mostly health care and retirement pensions, neither of which create economic growth. In fact, a society of elders may create economic stagnation, as we learn in the next section from the example of Japan.

15

POPULATION SHIFT
From Baby Boom to Elderpocalypse

LABOR

The population implosion has already begun in Japan. Its population peaked at about 130 million in 2005 and is now in decline, and at a surprisingly rapid rate. Why Japan? The answer is most likely 'urbanization,' as it's not a coincidence that Japan is one of the most urbanized nations in the world. That is, a higher proportion of Japanese citizens live in cities than in any other nation.

Indeed, Japanese women had fewer children in 2017 than in any year since 1899. Yes, *1899*. And assuming this trend continues then by 2100 Japan is forecast to have about *half* as many people as at the 2005 peak, only 65 million. If that does happen then of course the impact on the economy will be huge. It will be an elderpocalypse.

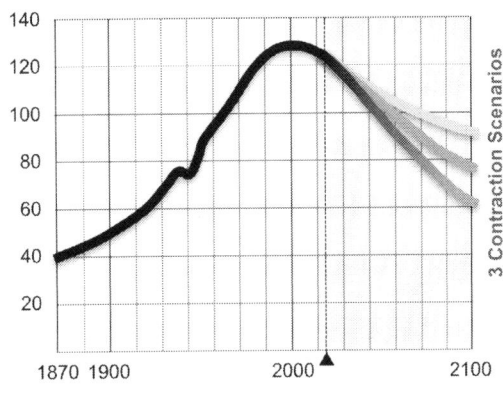

Japanese Population – Millions

But that's not necessarily a future topic either, since Japan's economy has been stagnant for decades. At least it has been underperforming from the perspective of the number one metric of the industrial economy, GDP growth. Since the elderly just don't consume as the young do, when Japan's workforce started shrinking then a slowdown in consumerism and a decline in tax revenues inevitably followed. Their households are already full of more stuff than they need, and most lose interest in collecting still more.

And since they're no longer earning taxable wages but they are consuming pensions and lots of health care, the drain on government funds increases as tax revenues decline, making for a brutal combination.

Thus, we see four critical factors operating together: *urbanization* leading to a *lower birth rate*, thus leading to *population decline*, thus leading to *tax revenue decline*, and combined with higher pension and health care costs for seniors.

This means that Japan's national budget is under extreme stress, and it's only going to get worse.

It might just be interesting as an anomaly, except that it's not an anomaly at all, because Japan isn't the only nation that's experiencing population decline and budget crisis. The count varies from year to year, but as many as 40 other nations are also experiencing population declines, and consequently all are beset by the same confluence of social and economic challenges. In Korea, the birthrate has dropped to the lowest in the world, 1.05 children per woman, and more than 3500 schools have closed since the 1980s.

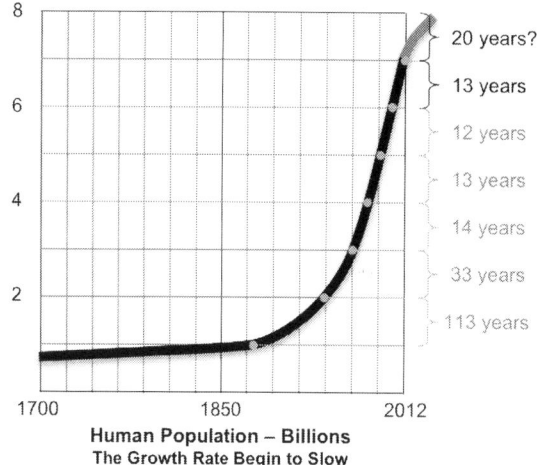

Human Population – Billions
The Growth Rate Begin to Slow

This provides us with a preview of what's in store for much of the world sooner, and probably the entire world later: as we complete the transition to full urbanization as Japan has already done, we should expect this to unfold everywhere.

And since industrial economics as practiced for the last 200 years seems to require a population boom to propel its growth, when the boom ends, which is what urbanization has effectively done, industrialism breaks down. If you doubt this just read the endless pile of news stories that lament Japan's lack of growth, and notice how this is depicted as 'underperformance,' 'malaise,' 'a disappointment,' or 'a failure of leadership' that a succession of political leaders have 'failed to overcome.' But it's not a political problem, it's a matter of fundamental social and economic behavior.

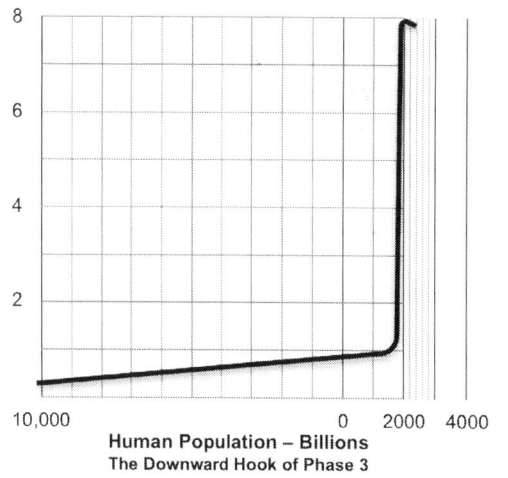

Human Population – Billions
The Downward Hook of Phase 3

If this is indeed a preview of coming attractions then we have arrived at yet another piece of evidence pointing to the conclusion that industrialism won't survive into the new population structure of Phase 3, and so the development of a new economic model is inevitable. Whatever the Phase 3 economy is going to be, it won't be the mass consumption industrial system we have lived within for the last two centuries.

16

EUROPEAN SHIFT
From Few to Fewer

LABOR

Other than Japan, many among the 40 nations that are experiencing population declines are in Europe, and particularly Eastern Europe. The birth rate everywhere from Germany to the east has dropped far below replacement level, and this combined with widespread emigration by young people has led to an overall population implosion throughout the region. In Lithuania, for example, the number of working aged people (defined as ages 15 to 64) declined by 25 percent between 1990 and 2015, and the number of 18 year olds has dropped by 33 percent since only 2011.

Why do they leave? They're searching for opportunity, of course, which can readily be found in the more dynamic economies of Western Europe, and for a richer social and cultural life as well.

Under these conditions, which have been described as 'demographic panic,' a whole suite of social and economic problems emerge, resulting in economic stresses that in turn create social and cultural pressures. Tax revenues decline, employers have difficulty filling jobs, and communities lose vitality as the average age of the population increases into the 40s and 50s.

It's not a coincidence that across Eastern Europe a new wave of authoritarian and nationalist politicians have emerged, characterized by demagogues who, as one would expect, promise to bring back the good old days. That they have attracted widespread support reflects how badly things have gone wrong, and indeed the loss of population presents a difficult economic situation because it inevitably slows the economy, and it also creates a sense of fatalism and evokes fear of a fading national identity.

Poland offers an interesting example of this problem. Unluckily situated between Germany and Russia, the Poles have seen their territory traversed by invading armies over the centuries, its borders drawn and redrawn by a series of conquerors from Napoleon to Hitler to Stalin. A sense of deep fatalism is even reflected in its national anthem, which begins with the rather depressing line, 'Poland has not yet perished,' as if it's inevitable one day. (It's also translated, equally depressingly, as 'Poland has not perished yet,' 'Poland is not lost,' 'Poland is not lost yet,' and 'Poland is not yet lost').

In roughly the same spirit, in 1946 the Hungarian intellectual Istvan Bibo published a pamphlet whose title clearly expresses its point: *The Misery of the Small States of Eastern Europe.* In it Bibo suggested that the memories of historical trauma would always linger, and would always provoke a deep sense of insecurity throughout the region. He seems to have been correct.

Forty years later things weren't much better, when in 1984 Czech writer Milan Kundera defined a small nation as 'one whose very existence may be put in question at any moment.' At the time he wrote this, Kundera had already emigrated to France, foreshadowing Eastern Europe's impending demographic demise, and also showing that the question of existence for the small nations of the region is no longer just a matter of external conquest, but also a function of low birth rates, departing families, and disintegrating communities. If everyone wants to leave, do we still have a nation?

And while immigration is possibly a partial solution to these demographic woes, social attitudes toward immigrants in most of these nations are not receptive, as immigrants are seen as a threat to national identity rather than as a solution to demographic decline. All of this places these nations in a trap from which there is no obvious means of exit.

•••

Our discussion of labor has traversed a lot of ground, from computer chips and robots to demographics, cities, and national fatalism. It's all connected, and it all converges on a single conclusion: during the next few decades we will transition to Phase 3, the shape of the population curve defining a new reality, and combined with the boom in robotics, assuring that industrialism will not continue as we have known it. We turn now to capital, where we will not surprisingly find further evidence of fundamental change.

'It is both emigration and the fear of immigration that best explain the rise of populism in Eastern Europe. The success of nationalist populism which feeds off a sense that a country's identity is under threat, is the outcome of the mass exodus of young people from the region combined with the prospect of large-scale immigration, which together set demographic alarm bells ringing.

Moving to the West was equivalent to rising in social status, and as a result, the eastern Europeans who stayed in their own countries started feeling like losers who had been left behind.'

Ivan Krastev
Foreign Affairs
May/June 2018

CAPITAL ▶ **17**

CAPITAL SHIFT
From Uncertainty to Even More

Capital is a complex and elusive topic, or in modern language, it's complicated. Karl Marx wrote his three massive volumes of *Das Capital* in an effort to understand what capital actually is, and while he researched and grappled for decades, in the end he had learned a tremendous amount but still had not fully mastered the subject. Today, one hundred and fifty years later we're not much better off, and the many different schools of economic thought, left, right, and center, have wide disagreements regarding nearly everything. Economists still struggle to understand the very complex workings of capital even as it's obviously fundamental to all economics. As the *Economist Magazine* pointed out recently, 'Economists understand even less about economic growth than they do about business cycles.' (April 24, 2018) This does not inspire great confidence.

The high degree of uncertainty also shows up in endless political and economic debates about taxes, the money supply, trade, and investment. It seems no one really knows for sure what will work, but they manage to get pretty excited about what they believe. Some are certain that government should print more money, others that the money supply should be restricted. Taxes should be raised; no, they should be lowered. Policies that seem to result in growth during one decade seem to increase poverty the next, or to function completely in a completely opposite way in a different country.

And now we have the economic impact of robots to consider: Will they result in wealth creation, or in wealth and social destruction? Or both? No one knows.

Today, our system is organized around the requirements of capital, which has the important characteristic that it transforms all production inputs into commodities, natural resources, climate, people, factories and homes and everything else is disposable fodder for the creation of more capital by capital.

This is the 'financialized' economy, but financialization isn't a word I made up, it's a technical term in economics that refers the explosive expansion of indebtedness and the creation of complex forms of finance in which loans are packaged and resold and then sold again in many forms of derivatives. Your home mortgage, car payment, credit card debt, even the monthly lease on your phone, they're all being packaged and sold in some form of a security instrument, and probably then repackaged into some form of a derivative security. As this occurs globally, a greater and greater proportion of economic activity is some form of debt. The total value of all derivatives is very hard to determine, but current estimates put it at between $500 and 600 trillion, an astonishing sum that's about 8x times greater than GDP.

Part of the problem is that capital is actually many different things. It's the money we save and then spend to buy things, of course, but it's also giant power plants and skyscrapers. It's specific forms of goods used in the production process to transform goods into other goods, goods into services, and services into services. Yes, it is complicated.

As we saw above, the process of automation replaces labor with capital, and so in health care, in manufacturing and warehousing and distribution, with self-driving cars, robot security guards and kitchen chefs, floor cleaners, and in countless other domains, every conceivable technology is being developed to replace human labor with machines, that is, with more capital.

This causes a growing concern that the mass deployment of robots will concentrate still more power in the hands of capital owners while significantly decreasing the value of labor, thereby worsening the imbalance between the wealthy one percent and the remaining ninety-nine percent. And how could increasing imbalance in wealth not lead to more social strife?

America's total private wealth is about $100 trillion. The wealthiest 1 percent of Americans hold nearly 39 percent of it (or $39 trillion, about $12 million each).

The next 9 percent holds a further 34 percent, a share that has crept steadily up since 1986, according to the World Inequality Database ($34 trillion, about $1.1 million each).

The middle 40 percent that would historically be considered middle class held 36 percent of the country's wealth in 1986, but now it's just 27 percent ($27 trillion, about $204,000 each).

The bottom 40 percent of Americans have a negative net worth, and thus many Americans are just one missed paycheck from crisis.

CBS/AP
June 16, 2018

18

COMMODITIZATION SHIFT
From Wealth to Commodity

The progressive development of technical expertise during the agricultural era made industry possible. The accumulation of knowledge about metallurgy and mechanics led to the creation of machines that transformed how farming was done, which in turn transformed the entire economy itself into something quite different from agriculture. Agriculture induced its own successor, just as industrialization is now doing.

This amazing transition from agricultural to industrial was not a planned or designed process, but one that occurred gradually as the aggregate and unexpected result of millions of actions and decisions by millions of people. As knowledge accumulated and industry came to predominate, ways of living and working quickly shifted because of the very nature of industry and way industry operated. Three of those changes were particularly significant.

First, the relationship between land and commerce changed fundamentally. Land, the term in economics that refers to all naturally occurring resources, had been the essential and precious resource of agriculture, and it was the basis of wealth. In the industrial model, however, land was degraded to a commodity, just more raw material for the industrial process. The essential provider that had been carefully nurtured for centuries suddenly became the object of mass exploitation. From 1800 onward the predictable consequence has been progressive environmental destruction.

Further, land, air, and water were not only raw materials but also waste depositories, so massive pollution became the norm. London's sky was black by coal smoke and the Thames a filthy waste dump that sometimes caught on fire. Later, millions of acres of Brazilian rain forest were bulldozed and as we learned above, the two rivers that fed the Aral Sea were diverted to cotton farms causing the world's fourth largest inland sea to dry up; it's now the Aralkum Desert. Countless other occurrences of damage and destruction which in social terms were also catastrophes were in economic terms merely normal to the functioning of the industrial process, necessary side effects of economic growth.

The nature of capital also changed. The great challenge of any nation's capital is that it serves two conflicting masters, foreign exchange for import and export, and internal markets for credit and currency. Since industrialism requires growth, and growth requires exports, and exports require that currencies compete in international currency markets, rather than protecting citizens from the ups and downs of market swings within a nation, currency management by governments must focus on protecting the external balance of payments. It is consequently the internal poor who suffer most.

The relationship between people and commerce changed as well, and in nearly the same way. Prior to 1800, a broadly held social contract assured most people of sufficient food except under the most extreme shortages, a universal understanding of shared responsibility. Under industrialism, workers became 'labor' and their efforts were also commoditized. People became replaceable components in the manufacturing process, and as a consequence poverty was no longer considered to be a structural problem of society and a shared responsibility to address, but came to be understood as simply their own fault, because they were lazy or undereducated.

In essence, then, all three factors, land, labor, and capital, have been transformed by entrepreneurial capitalism into replaceable commodities, subject to exploitation and substitution, and thus subject to the ups and downs of the industrialism's booms and busts. During the agricultural era, the structure of society shaped commerce, but the emergence of industrial capital as the central axis now dominates the social process.

In the digital era, a quite different pattern is likely to emerge, one in which people and their creativity will again play a central role.

19

DEBT SHIFT BOMB
From Products to Financialization

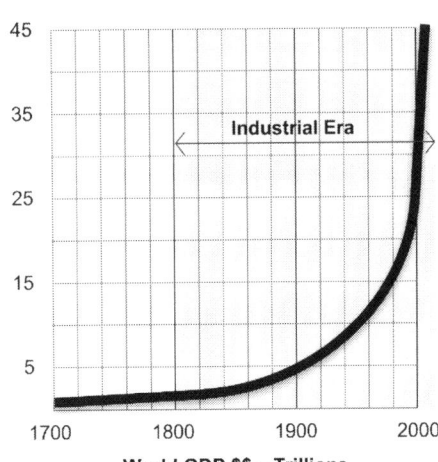

World GDP $$ – Trillions

Globalization Hits
Tanzania
2017

Used clothing imports:
540 million items (73%)

New clothing imports:
180 million items (24%)

New clothing
manufactures:
20 million items (3%)

The Economist
June 2, 2018

CAPITAL The latest wave of economic globalization that now dominates capitalism has produced astonishing increases in the value of capital, particularly as measured by GDP, which the graph to the left certainly makes clear. The nine-fold increase since 1900 is stunning.

But it's also produced some surprising side effects.

A small example is the trade dispute over the tiny $18 million Rwandan market for used clothing. Rwandan import duties protect local producers, but the US, in a fit of bullying pique, objects. The background to the story explains the broader process of economic globalization, which is also called 'neoliberalism.' To become eligible to receive foreign loans and investment, many nations agree to reduce or eliminate protective tariffs, thus opening their markets to global business. As a result, African nations became heavily indebted while also losing important industries at home. Ghana lost 80 percent of its textile manufacturing jobs, Kenya lost half its firms, and Tanzania now imports 97% of its clothing (see the sidebar to the left).

The capital was intended to help these countries develop, but as you know significant portions of the money was siphoned off by dictators and their cronies, enriching themselves but impoverishing their fellow citizens. Today Africa remain starkly underdeveloped compared with the rest of the world.

The debts are still due, though, sucking value out of the African economy. In fact, indebtedness is now the common condition worldwide, showing the most recent developmental stage of industrial capitalism. Debt unwisely assumed caused the 2008 financial collapse, and a full depression was avoided only when governments created vast amounts of money they called 'quantitative easing,' an obscure name chosen so few would understand what was really happening, and all to prop up consumption and avoid a repeat of 1929. In the US alone, the national bank created $3.5 *trillion* of new money to avert a total meltdown.

The underlying dynamic of industrial capitalism has thus shifted from a focus on manufacturing products for consumption, to manufacturing debt to keep the consumption party rolling. Now we live in a global empire of debt, or seen in another way, a 'debt shift bomb' that's liable to explode again at any moment, just as it did in 2008.

Consider what has happened in China, for example. The 2008 recession hit China's manufacturing firms very hard, as exports dropped by about 30 percent almost overnight. In most nations that would have led to a catastrophe, and indeed by some accounts 20 to 30 million Chinese jobs were lost. However, the state stepped in and launched a series of huge infrastructure building projects to re-employ people, but at the cost of incurring enormous debts. China's total national indebtedness, combining public and private, rose from 144 percent of national GDP in 2007 to 245 percent of national GDP in 2014, and by 2018 it was up to a gigantic 300 percent. GDP grew fast; debt grew even faster.

Globally, the scary total debt figure is now above $200 *trillion*, about 3x global GDP. How will all that debt ever be repaid? It probably won't, thereby constituting the trigger for some future crisis.

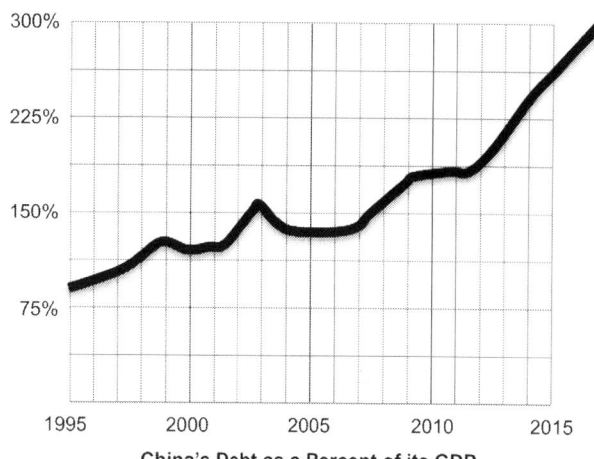

China's Debt as a Percent of its GDP

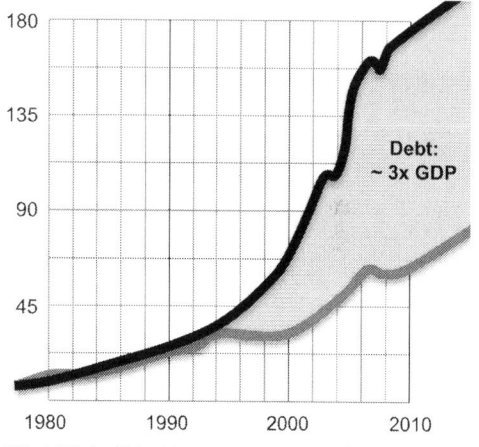

World Debt (Black) and GDP (Gray) $$ – Trillions

What all this tells us is that the economic system may have *already* moved past industrialism, based instead now on movement of capital: we have a financialized economy. Need more evidence? Total currency exchange transactions, seeking to make money purely by speculating on money, average about $5 trillion per day, 22 times greater than the productive GDP of about $220 billion per day. Yes, the system has moved on already.

20

FINANCIALIZATION SHIFT
From Capital, More Capital

CAPITAL

This shift to financialization began during the 1980s, by which time the lessons of the 1920s and 30s had largely been forgotten and the protective regulations enacted then were undone, bringing capital itself back to the focal point. US President Ronald Reagan led noisy and belligerent public rallies at which he and his outraged constituents demanded that the US federal budget 'must be balanced,' but during the eight years of his presidency Reagan himself managed to submit a balanced budget to the Congress not a single time, disclosing the deep contradiction between the homespun rhetoric and the policy. In fact the policy was capital and debt.

Twenty years later George Bush carried the same message and then did the same thing, cutting taxes and starting the disastrous and hideously expensive Iraq war in the very same year, further deepening US federal debt. During his eight years in office the total debt doubled to $11 trillion, and then it expanded by another $8 trillion under President Obama. In 2017 President Trump forced another massive tax cut through the US Congress that will add yet another $1 trillion to American debt, and by 2020 the US debt is forecast to be about $28 trillion.

So debt is in fashion, not only in the US but globally, and in this game the debt makers play by their own rules. For instance, during Greek's recent financial crisis, the U.S. banking firm Goldman Sachs aided the Greek government by selling it derivatives to help manage its debts, but then played the other side as well and sold a different derivative to another client that would deliver profits *only in the event of the Greek government's bankruptcy*. Goldman, of course, earned handsome fees from both sides.

Many of the world's big debts will never be repaid in full, creating a perpetual cycle of interest payments, which for capital owners is an exceptional method of creating still more capital, but for many debtors is a lifelong trap. The great problem with debt, both private and public, is that the requirements of debt servicing take control of an individual's life (private debt) and of public finance (public debt), and in the latter case democracy itself is undermined. Choice is destroyed when debt accumulates, for individuals as for nations, and then there's nothing left to vote on.

Logic tells us that there's a limit to how much debt any society can carry, and indeed the historian Ferdinand Braudel has noted that when financial speculation takes over any empire, it often marks the beginning of its demise. This may be our story now, and so while somehow the debt binge will taper off or just collapse, it's sure to be a gut-wrenching restructuring. Financialization in its current form thus cannot go on indefinitely, but is the end in sight? Perhaps not yet, but soon.

Unraveling this tangled mess will occupy the bankers and ministers for decades to come, and it may even become a triggering event for the definitive shift to digitalization, the Big Shift.

And now into this giant ocean of uncertainty enters digital money, cryptocurrency, which invites still more unknowns into the conversation. Indeed, many economists now believe that the very nature of capital is about to undergo a major shift because cryptocurrencies are created by people, not by governments, and what does it mean when anyone can create a currency?

In fact no one know what it means. But as with so many other technological innovations, the approach we take is to create it because we can, and then we'll see what happens.

21

BLOCKCHAIN SHIFT
From Paper to Digital

CAPITAL

Suppose that there was a form of money, useful money that people would happily accept in trade, but it wasn't issued by any government, it was instead was created by anyone who wanted to. What then? This is what the Bitcoin experiment is intended to find out. It's a new form of capital, digital money, (also called cybercurrency or cryptocurrency), intended to replace paper money.

Why would anyone want to do that? Because as we have seen above, nations have the unfortunate tendency to print too much money, thereby making their currencies less valuable, which of course is bad for everyone who holds that currency. Do you remember the tragic photos of the 1920s when appalling inflation meant that people needed a wheelbarrow full of money to buy a loaf of bread? Runaway inflation happens when the government creates oversupply in order to buy more of whatever it wants, whether that's guns and aircraft carriers, jobs and urban infrastructure, or foreign exchange.

The dream of a digital currency as the remedy has existed for a long time, but it wasn't until a long list of conceptual and technical barriers were solved that it became possible. The blockchain, a set of techniques used to represent information in computer code using nearly immutable records is the key, and the blockchain is significant not only for Bitcoin but also for many other uses, and thus it appears that the blockchain approach is likely to become just as disruptive as the internet itself has proven to be.

The invention of both blockchain and Bitcoin is attributed to Satoshi Nakamoto, but no actual person with the name 'Nakamoto' has ever made a public appearance, which has led to speculation that Nakamoto may be a pseudonym for a person or even a group. Given the potentially revolutionary nature of Bitcoin, opting for anonymity was probably a pretty smart choice.

'Cryptocurrencies are everything you don't understand about money combined with everything you don't understand about computers.'

John Oliver
Comedian (and economist)

Most explanations of what blockchains are and could become are expressed through mountains of unrecognizable and unhelpful jargon, but that's only because it's an entirely new language, one that's still being invented, to describe an entirely new capability whose implications are still being discovered.

For instance, since blockchain records are nearly immutable, they're ideal for storing public records, because immutability prevents fraud, theft, and corruption. Hence, property ownership records stored on blockchains in corruption-prone cities would significantly improve protection for owners, preventing illegal land seizures that are today common across many parts of the world. Blockchains also make complex business transactions easier to accomplish, and as described to the right, they therefore facilitate trade. They also authenticate identity, ownership, and even represent abstract qualities including 'trust,' 'reliability,' and 'reputation' in digital form. The United Nations, for example, is developing blockchain-based identity records for stateless inhabitants of its many refugee camps, which will enable people who would otherwise be trapped to emigrate, get jobs, and rebuild their lives.

Blockchain-based 'tokens' are evolving into a new form of securities, smart securities in which the rules for ownership and transfer are written into the design of the token itself, thereby preventing fraud while promoting transparency and compliance.

What blockchain technology lacks at present is a friendly and easy-to-understand public face. But then it wasn't so long ago that we didn't know what 'TCP-IP' was, or the 'world wide web,' a 'browser,' a 'search engine,' 'wifi,' 'bluetooth,' 'emoji,' or 'app store.' Now they're all common knowledge and part of everyday life, and when blockchains fulfill their potential then today's obscure and unrecognizable language will mature and be simplified to become as familiar as other everyday technologies have become.

Bitcoin and the blockchains they're based on are just two among many technologies that are having profound influence on our future, as we will see next.

According to the World Economic Forum, the cost of processing trade documents is as much as a fifth the cost of transport. Removing administrative blockages in supply chains could do more to boost international trade than eliminating tariffs.

According to the United Nations, full digitalization of trade paperwork could raise exports from Asia-Pacific countries alone by $250 billion per year.

The Economist
March 24, 2018

22

TECHNOLOGY SHIFT
From Knowledge to Innovation

CAPITAL

Every week it seems that there are still more announcements about major advances across science, technology, and commerce, and thus our list of amazing breakthroughs has to be constantly revised because the new, the awesome, and the previously unknown have become reality.

These advances in knowledge represent another significant form of capital that society uses to further transform all facets of work and life. But knowledge as capital differs from money and machinery capital because an unlimited number of users can benefit from the very same unit of knowledge without diluting its value for any of them. Further, through its use, knowledge often grows *more* valuable, and when it's consumed it isn't destroyed, but rather it's often enhanced and improved.

Money, machinery, and knowledge thus compose a compelling triad of quite different forms of capital that, when brought together, propel the economy forward by leveraging land's resources and peoples' capabilities.

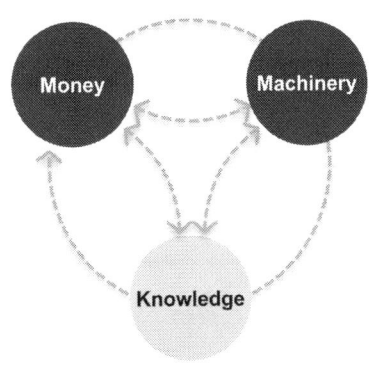

Forms of Capital

When new knowledge is usefully applied it also becomes something else – *innovation* – which is the driving force of both economic and social change, and a topic we'll discuss at length in Part 3. As noted above, the demise of industrialism is not due to its failures, but rather to its amazing success at innovation, at creating such an abundance of both new stuff and new knowledge. Technology, of course, accelerates the creation of both, so much so that now the entire economy is reorganizing itself around digitalization, marking the shift to the digital economy.

While this book is not intended as an inventory of all the cool (and frighteningly uncool) innovations that the digital shift is bringing to daily reality, it would be an oversight not to at least mention some of them. Thus, in addition to chips and robots which we've already discussed, these technologies are already having major disruptive impacts:

- *Virtual Reality (VR):* Immersive simulations enable us to engage with information in new ways, changing us from passive spectators to active participants.

- *Augmented Reality (AR):* By bringing computer generated information into our perceptual field we enhance perception and decision making.

- *Machine Learning and Artificial Intelligence:* Computers are programmed to learn and predict, thereby advancing beyond simply processing information to making decisions and creating new possibilities.

- *Drones:* Combining advanced sensors, remote monitoring, and super efficient motors, drones are coming in the air and water.

- *Big Data:* Computers are now so powerful that they can study millions of data points to identify solutions and patterns that simply could not have previously have been recognized.

- *Holograms:* Many applications in communications, advanced product design, and virtual presence apply holograms to enable much more effective visualization of complexity.

- *3D Printing:* 3D printing devices make fully customized products and execute much more complex designs than traditional manufacturing. (See Section 62)

- *Quantum Computing:* By exploiting the essential characteristics of matter, computing devices of the future may be orders of magnitude more powerful than today's, enabling an entire universe of new applications and possibilities.

- *Supercomputing:* The global arms race in supercomputing between China, Japan, Europe, and the US finds each vying to build faster and faster machines, which are used for super complex large scale simulations. From 2005 to 2020 hardware speeds are projected to increase by a factor of 3000, with each step forward enabling huge scientific advances.

Automotive designers at Ford are now using hologram technology to speed up the process of designing new cars.

Motor Trend
September 21, 2017

China's second largest ecommerce firm JD.com, has implemented a drone delivery network in 100 rural Chinese villages that is already providing same day delivery at a cost of about 80% less than using a truck and driver.

The Economist
June 9, 2018

There are of course many more technologies to consider, each potentially disruptive because each enables entirely new ways of making, doing, experiencing, and/or learning, all examples of capital applied to creation, all possible because of the steadily increasing power of computer chips, and all demonstrating the synergy between money, machinery, and knowledge.

23

HEALTH CARE SHIFT
From Standardized to Customized

CAPITAL

The rising cost to provide health care is one of the great challenges of modern society, and of course with the steady increase in the number of elderly citizens in all countries these costs will inevitably rise.

In the U.S., health care costs already consume about 18 percent of the national GDP, and they're increasing each year. This is considerably more than any other developed nation spends, even though American health outcomes are not better, and in many cases they're worse.

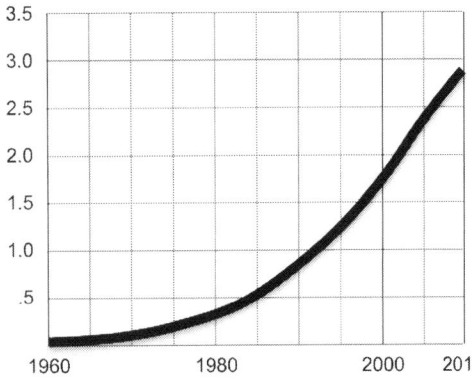

USA Health Care Expenditures – $ Trillions

In addition to systemic flaws, chronic inefficiency, and inherent problems with for-profit health care, another reason for rising costs not only in the US but worldwide is the continuing development and application of new technologies and new treatments. For example, a da Vinci robotic surgery system costs about $3 million for the robot, and adds at least $3000 to the cost of each operation. But studies have shown that the robotic surgery patients have shorter hospital stays and less blood loss, so the extra cost provides benefits that are definitely influencing the choices of both patients and physicians. Constant pressure for the newest and best treatments and the accompanying machinery is thus a major driver of increasing cost.

And of course a huge range of even more advanced technologies are being developed for health care, just as they are for every other kind of business and activity. Here's a sampling:

- *Big data and predictive analytics:* Now that health records are digital, we have the ability to assemble very large sets of data on thousands of millions of individuals to discover patterns of patient behavior and to analyze the results from different forms of treatment. Thus, instead of preferences and guesswork, physicians and patients now have the capacity to learn precisely what the best forms of treatment are, and the necessary behaviors to attain the best outcomes. Consequently, the field of 'predictive analytics' is enabling health care providers to make much better care recommendations and prescriptions for their patents.

- *Exoskeletons:* It's not all in software, though, as new types of hardware and devices are being developed such as exoskeletons, structural support systems that enable people with disabilities or amputated limbs to have a much fuller range of experiences, restoring mobility and dexterity and thus enabling them to live much fuller lives.

- *Artificial Body Parts:* About one million knee and hip replacements are done in the U.S. each year, and scientists are now working to create artificial body parts using tools ranging from genetic engineering to 3D printing, innovations may one day help restore health to those suffering major organ damage or failure, and may also extend the lives of patients for years or even decades.

- *Customized Medicines:* Science can now map your entire genome (see the next section) and gain a huge amount of information about your specific body chemistry and metabolism, and can also assess the results from millions of medication doses taken by millions of patients. Putting the two together brings us to the era of customized medicine, treatments formulated specifically for your exact requirements and body chemistry.

Most of these technologies increase costs, but they also provide better treatment than was ever before possible. Thus, as the world's population continues to age, the demands on health care systems will continue to increase, technologies will continue to advance, and thus complexity and costs will continue to rise as well.

In addition to creating new treatments and components, science is now also creating the tools to alter the basic design patterns of life by manipulating the gene, potentially treating conditions before they arise.

'The U.S. Food and Drug Administration has approved an artificial-intelligence based disease screening software that does not need a clinician to interpret the results. The computer program analyses digital images of a patient's retina to detect diabetic retinopathy. The software correctly identified about 88% of patients with and without the disease.'

Science Magazine
April 20, 2018

24

GENE SHIFT
From Evolution to Engineering

CAPITAL

Life on Earth first developed about 3.8 billion years ago, and although we have no idea how this happened we nevertheless mark this as the point at which evolution began. Evolution's medium is the gene, and its tools are random mutation, natural selection, and environmental change that normally unfold over tens of thousands and millions of years. The single celled organism has become the plants and animals and insects that blanket the Earth, along with us.

And for millennia humans have been influencing the design of life through selective breeding, transforming wild plants and animals into domesticated species that provide our food supply. And now with the development of biotechnology and genetic engineering, our ability to shape the very structures and patterns of life has advanced to a new level.

We already create clones, exact genetic replicas of living animals, and we are not far from the era of 'designer babies,' children whose qualities and features are selected as a matter of choice and design rather than acquired through sexual reproduction. Once again science has attained the reach of science fiction, and the prospects are both fascinating and frightening.

From the perspective of the Big Shift, where the focus is on identifying the factors that are driving fundamental change in society and also considering their implications, there can hardly be anything more fundamental than the possibility of altering the basic code of life. Biotechnology and genetic engineering thus have the possibility to change the direction of human society and civilization in ways that few other changes can match, forever altering the direction of evolution itself. 3+ billion years of evolutionary history shifts now that engineers have the capacity to shape the future of life.

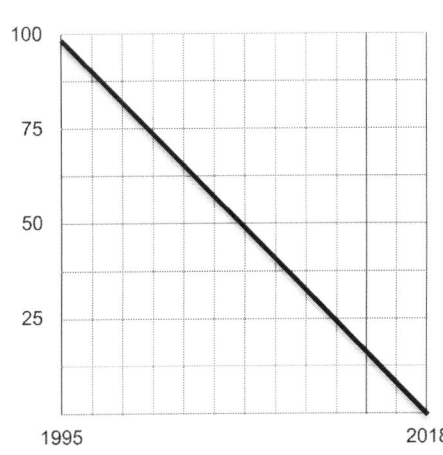

Cost of one Genetic Sequence - $ Millions

It's important to note that biotechnology is possible only because of the incredible and increasing power of computer technology, the ubiquitous chip that makes all form of data collection and processing so fast and easy. Without modern computing, genetic engineers would be working as their grandparents did, identifying preferred traits of plants and animals and waiting through natural reproductive cycles to see the results.

But now private firms can map your entire genome for $100 or so, and already more than 25 million people have done so.

The CRISPR genetic engineering technique (it stands for Clustered Regularly Interspaced Short Palindromic Repeats) accelerates this process even more, compressing years, decades, and millennia into hours and days in the lab. Dr. Jennifer Doudna is one of the inventor/creators of CRISPR explains it this way:

Number of People in DNA Registries, millions

> What makes this different is that the tool is precise and programmable. We can now change a single letter in the three billion base pairs of the human genome. Ever since the discovery of the structure of DNA in the 1950s, scientists have been dreaming about being able to rewrite that code. What if you could correct mutations that cause disease or introduce new and beneficial traits into a species? Now we have a tool that can do that. Now you can simply splice in a trait for a bigger nose, disease resistance, better nutrition, whatever. You can do it precisely in one generation and get exactly what you want. This is changing the way modern biology is being practiced.
>
> 'The Ultimate Life Hacker: A Conversation with Jennifer Doudna.' *Foreign Affairs*, May/June 2018

The impact on human society is certain to be enormous, but like the arrival of mass scale robotics, the outcomes are utterly uncertain. Soon labs will patent and sell the genes needed to make your child a Mozart, or a great athlete, or a world class mathematician. But as many of these experiments may go awry, the result may also be suffering and despair. We are indeed entering a new era, entirely uncharted and unpredictable, but undoubtedly impactful.

25

WARFARE SHIFT
From Battlefield to Cyberspace

In 1519 Leonardo da Vinci sought a job with the Duke of Milan, and in his application letter he described himself as an unparalleled inventor of military machinery. Among his many claims, he wrote, 'I have types of cannon, most convenient and easily portable, with which to hurl small stones almost like a hail-storm; and the smoke from the cannon will instill a great fear in the enemy on account of the grave damage and confusion.' He got the job.

It's sad but true that the history of warfare runs parallel with the development of technology, for armies have always been patrons of innovation. This of course where we get the concept of the Arms Race, the contest to develop more efficient ways to threaten, kill, and destroy.

The tank and military aircraft were World War I innovations, radar and huge bombers and rockets in World War II, the atom bomb and the smart missile and the smart bullet and spy satellites in the Cold War, and more recently drones and smart bombs and guided missiles and IEDs. Similarly, the development of the internet was funded by the US military's venture investment arm, DARPA, because of its usefulness for military communications.

Of course the common element in all these examples is technology, and now soldiers, sailors, and airmen are all being augmented but also replaced by powerful, destructive, thinking machines that compete on the high-tech-enabled digital battlefield. What, then, will the consequences of the continuing refinement of computer technology mean for warfare? And what will the unscrupulous genetic engineers create in the way of super soldiers or killer viruses to impact upon the future of civilization?

Neither prospect is appealing, for both undoubtedly mean more robots at war and thus more violence and death. In 2014 President Obama joked that the U.S. military was developing a suit like the one in the Iron Man movies, only to learn afterwards that a project to do that really existed, and there was already a working prototype. Change is accelerating.

Soon entire armies of 'killer robots' (killbots), automatons, drones, and remotely-controlled super weaponry will be racing across battlefields and cities, and so once again fiction becomes fact as technology moves from the screenplay and cinema into the real theaters of real war. Super-soldier-suits, smart weapons, satellite-guidance, all are already elements in the modern arsenal, and computers are essential to all of them, so much so that the U.S. military's newest branch is 'Cyber Command,' whose mission is to both defend the military's information networks and to attack the networks of others.

And the cyber war has already begun. Iran's nuclear development program was attacked in 2010 by Stuxnet, a computer virus developed, apparently, by U.S. and Israeli computer scientists. Covertly installed into at least 14 Iranian nuclear weapons development sites, it caused machinery to malfunction and then self destruct. The success of Stuxnet and subsequent cyber weapons alerted everyone that critical infrastructures such as power plants and power transmission systems are vulnerable to cyber attack. And so, we learned in 2016, are elections.

Given that society now depends so completely on technology, and given the inherent vulnerability of technology to intrusion and hijacking, cyberwar will undoubtedly play a major role in all future conflicts, bringing to the conventional fields of arms a high-tech sibling, the war in cyberspace.

Cyber weaponry is, sadly and ironically, the application of capital to achieve the destruction of capital.

Blockchains, cryptocurrencies, new knowledge, robots, genetic engineering, all of these are forms of capital that are, as we can easily see, introducing change into the structure of the economy and society, and thus they are on the leading edge of the transformation to the digital economy.

ENTREPRENEUR ▶ # 26

ENTREPRENEUR SHIFT
From Taxi to Uber

The fourth of the four factors of production in classical economics is entrepreneurism, the process of creating new businesses. This form of innovation is of course central to capitalism, as it is the means by which change is introduced into the marketplace by entrepreneurs who organize land, labor, and capital to create new technologies and new companies.

Uber is a lovely example, the digital disruption of the staid and unchanged taxi industry by entrepreneurs who recognized how to use smart phone technology to transform an unpleasant experience into an easy one. To fulfill its apparently enormous potential Uber requires a massive amount of capital, and this is addressed by the shared stock corporation, an industrial era invention that provides entrepreneurs with the means to aggregate huge amounts of capital within a manageable organizational structure. Similarly, the practice of franchising aligns the interests of local entrepreneurs with global brands to leverage the strengths and advantages of both. Auto makers, beverage makers, restaurants, and hotel brands use the franchise model to broaden their capital base and enlarge their pools of management.

During the industrial era it would require a staff of possibly thousands of people to build and operate the factories and offices, and the enterprise that aspired to operate globally would have to create its own massive management structure to keep the whole thing organized, building towering offices to house them, and hiring legions of clerks and secretaries to support them. The great steel and oil companies, the auto and aircraft companies, the food and consumer goods makers, all built and ran giant factories and offices employing tens of thousands. At its peak, more than 85,000 worked at Ford's enormous River Rouge plant outside of Detroit. Giant conglomerates then arose by combining many types of businesses in into a single megacorporation.

The triumph of industrialism brought the era of the MBA, and the biggest firms were admired for the professionalism of their highly trained managements.

It's much different today. Since nearly every role of management and operations can be outsourced, from human resources to accounting, finance, marketing, and advertising, now a small team of entrepreneurs can create a giant global corporation with a tiny staff. All facets of production and distribution can be outsourced, and they don't even need to buy computers, servers, software, and the services needed to operate even a complex tech business, because they, too, can also be rented. Indeed, this one of Amazon.com's most profitable business. Consequently, the amount of money needed to establish even a global business is shrinking rapidly. What money is required tends to go directly into marketing to build market awareness and market share.

Consequently, giant and not-very-nimble Corporation X now finds itself in a very tough competition with a handful of tech-savvy programmers whose innovative business model is getting started with next to no capital at all.

Using these new digital economy tools and techniques, an endless stream of new companies will be created to bring new ideas and technologies to market, and with the emergence of new forms of money such as Bitcoin and new methods of capital formation such as the ICO (Initial Coin Offering, described in the following section), entrepreneurs will have even more versatile tools for capital raising, which could also stimulate broader participation in the entrepreneurial process, thus setting the stage for an entrepreneurial renaissance.

Volkswagen is building Rwanda's first auto assembly plant, even though the total market for new cars in the country is only about 3,000 per year, and past attempts have ended in 'monumental failure.' So how will Volkswagen succeed?

The business model calls for VW to build cars for its own car sharing service, a la Uber, and then sell them in the used market a few years later.

VW thus wishes to avoid becoming 'Corporation X' by out-ubering Uber. It shows they're paying attention.

The Economist
June 30, 2018

27

FUNDING SHIFT
From IPO to ICO

ENTREPRENEUR

When a company, whether young or old, needs to raise capital that, too, can now be done in new ways.

Crowdfunding is a method of raising money directly from individuals who prepay for a product or service, or who donate their support for a good idea or a good cause. The amounts raised through crowdsourcing are usually modest, but now blockchain technologies have created a new way to assemble capital in huge amounts through the 'Initial Coin Offering,' or ICO, and so we see that the full range of capital raising approaches are experiencing digital disruption.

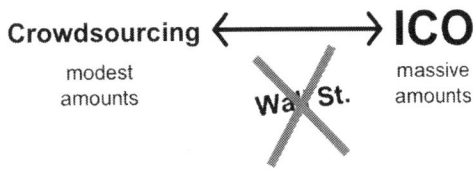

Direct Forms of Capital Formation for Entrepreneurs

ICO investors exchange money for ownership just like buying stock, except that unlike the stock market of an Initial Public Offering (IPO), the transaction is managed directly between investor and company, and it's all recorded on a blockchain. Since no Wall Street middle man is required for either form of funding, we observe that crowdfunding disrupts the industry of small scale finance while the ICO has the potential to disrupt the big business of the big Wall Street and Silicon Valley financiers. Yes, even the bankers are being disrupted.

As these approaches become common we observe that two essential elements of entrepreneurism have abruptly shifted: capital formation through crowdsourcing, ICOs, and new approaches that haven't been invented yet make it fabulously easy to raise money, and the outsourcing of nearly all aspects of business operations means that any company can scale up from fledgling idea to full operations in unheard of speed.

While in the past the founders of a start-up company had to spend far too much of their time raising capital, now they're be able to devote much more time to building their businesses and making impact in the market.

Since these tools make starting a company easier than it has ever been, we should expect that they will further accelerate the formation of new companies, and so we should expect hundreds of thousands of new firms to be born in the coming years not only in the developed nations, but worldwide. This explosion of entrepreneurism could well become a transformative force enabling millions to benefit from yet another wave of innovations, surely adding more force to the shifting structure of the marketplace by disrupting existing businesses.

That is, they will transform established business models and disrupt industries using insights, creativity, and technology. This will mean new competitors for established firms, thereby increasing the rate of creative destruction across the marketplace, further accelerating the page of change. (For more on business model innovation see Section 64.)

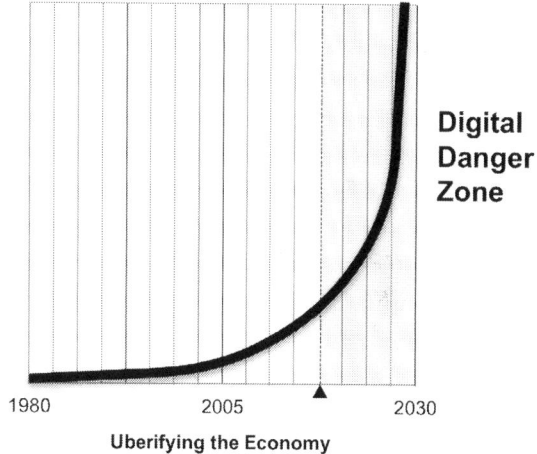

Digital Danger Zone

We might call this 'Uberifying' the entire economy, and as leaders of established firms come to recognize that we have entered the 'digital danger zone' due to the threats they face from the potent combination of new technology and new entrepreneurism, they, too will adopt these new management behaviors and practices, which will of course only serve to further accelerate the process.

1980   2005   2030

Uberifying the Economy

Industrialism has hatched the digital offspring that will supplant it, and the new waves of entrepreneurism will impact not only on the Earth-bound economy, but in space as well.

28

OUTER SPACE SHIFT
From Earth Economy to Space Commerce

ENTREPRENEUR

Some of the most compelling new entrepreneurial stories are about companies created to operate off the Earth, not in existing markets but in brand new ones. The most famous companies, Elon Musk's Space X and Jeff Bezos' Blue Origin are in the rocketry business, Bigelow Aerospace has already delivered an inflatable space habitat to the International Space Station, and Virgin Galactic is developing spacecraft for tourism.

But already there are many more of these enterprises than you may realize. Dozens of firms are developing ambitious plans and brilliant technologies to enable ventures that will mine the moon and asteroids for valuable minerals, build space colonies and space hotels, and explore and inhabit Mars. While such ventures were once exclusively the realm of science fiction they are now rapidly becoming quite real and very capital intensive entrepreneurial efforts that could also transform the economy on Earth.

Commerce in space isn't new, however, as the satellite industry has been providing valuable telecommunications services for decades. Today's farmers rely on observation and navigation satellites, and so do you whenever you use a GPS device. Since the maps on your cell phone rely on GPS, this means that you benefit directly from space technology every time you get directions from Google, or call an Uber. Satellites are also essential to weather forecasting, emergency preparedness, and disaster relief, and to Earth science and astronomy. The revenue of the global satellite industry in 2016 totaled an impressive $260 billion, having doubled during the course of only a decade, and we can expect the growth rate to accelerate. Even under the most modest of scenarios, by 2030 space commerce will likely be a trillion dollar industry, and it could be much more.

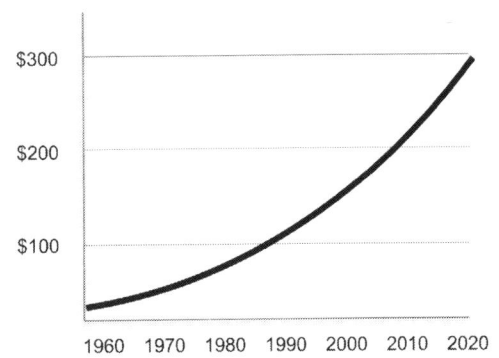

Global Revenue from Space Commerce
Billions of Dollars

As these new commercial efforts in space become successful they will change the way we think about business, about international relations and geopolitics, and especially how we think about humanity's place on the Earth and in the cosmos.

Space commerce at a larger scale could also change the structure of Earth's economy in fundamental ways by altering the supply of critical natural resources, which, as we have noted already, are obviously finite.

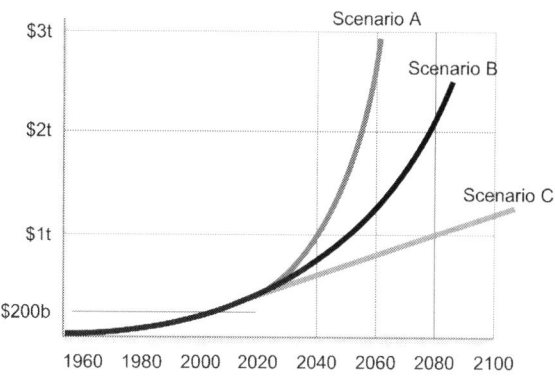

Global Revenue from Space Commerce, 3 Scenarios
Trillions of Dollars

What other applications of space-based technologies will transform the economy? And in what ways? The possibilities are startling. For example, consider the impact that extended living in space will have on human evolution. Since life in space and outside of Earth's protective atmosphere induces permanent change to human DNA, those living off-world will likely if unintentionally create new branches on the tree of human evolution. The terms 'transhuman' (still human, but with exceptional new capabilities) and 'posthuman' (evolved into new species, branching from the human line) have been invented to describe the new genomes of those whose DNA has diverged so significantly from human DNA as to constitute new species.

Large scale space commerce enterprises could easily be the norm within thirty years, and it's plausible that humanity will colonize local portions of our galaxy within a century. When that happens perhaps someone will write a book about the shift from the digital economy to the 'cosmo-economy.'

And perhaps new species will emerge within a few centuries, thus marking new waves of shifts brought forth by the consequences of life and commerce in outer space, thereby further transforming our ideas about human life, and introducing emerging fields into our awareness such as 'cosmo-politics.'

For the present, however, we have much to concern ourselves with in the shift from industrial to digital, and with the resulting changes in conventional, Earth-bound geopolitics.

29

GEOPOLITICS SHIFT
From Nation-State to Non-State

ENTREPRENEUR

The primacy and sovereignty of the nation-state has been an accepted principle in international relations since 1648, when the structure of international law was established that upholds the independence of nations as the ultimate authorities over what goes on within their own territories.

In the digital economy, however, national sovereignty is threatened by the new category of entrepreneurial forces called 'non-states,' which have found the means to exert tremendous and fragmenting influence over the nation-state. Yes, digital disruption has significantly eroded the capacity of the nation to sustain its immutable sovereignty, and thus the massive transition of the Big Shift impacts not only the economic structure of society, but also on the nation-state itself as the organizing principle of global society.

Among the specific new forces having enormous impact are two forms of non-state actors, criminal gangs that operate globally and digitally with no regard for national borders, and terrorist organizations. Criminal entrepreneurs move drugs, slaves, and contraband, and now that kidnapping is a billion dollar business they're into that, too. (Today, you really can buy insurance to cover the costs of kidnapping and ransom.) And while gangs wreak havoc, terrorists wreak death, destruction, and fear globally not as agents of any nation, but agents of ideology.

At the same time, the multi-national corporation shows less interest in defining its identity with reference to any nation, but sees itself more and more as an economic entity that operates outside of the nation-state system. Corporations park profits wherever they can pay the least in taxes, operate where there is the least oversight and regulation, and show much loyalty to shareholders but little to citizens or governments. Indeed, nation-states are no longer considered to be enablers of commercial success, they're barriers to be avoided or evaded.

As this comment from Woodrow Wilson shows, the corporation once followed the state, but now the state follow the corporation:

'Since trade ignores national boundaries, and the manufacturer insists on having the world as a market, the flag of his nation must follow him, and the doors of the nations which are closed against him must be battered down.'

Woodrow Wilson

The super-rich also pursue lifestyles of state-avoidance, owning assets worldwide but keeping their ownership secret from the state to avoid taxation, while employing vast armies of quasi-legal banks and lawyers to hide assets worth trillions. Holding two or three passports, they jet from nation to nation with loyalty to none. Since the super-rich are amassing control of an ever-greater proportion of all assets, their non-state attitude has a major impact on tax revenues, and on social norms. The stateless super-rich thus constitute an entirely new class of non-citizenry.

At the opposite end of the non-state, non-citizen spectrum are those who are stateless not by choice, but because their nation has disintegrated. Millions live in sprawling refugee camps surrounding the remains of Syria and across northeastern Africa, and because they do not hold valid passports they are also non-citizens, brutally trapped in statelessness and poverty.

Another factor that may drive further erosion of nation-states is the blockchain, and the 'computational currencies' that blockchains enable. Since they're forms of money created specifically to avoid nation-state currencies, if and when they come to be used widely then fiat currencies and national governments will exert even less influence. Bitcoin and its offspring may even lead to the formation of new nations based outside of any national territory. Where will that be? We'll certainly see attempts to create new ocean-going self-sovereignties inhabited by those who wish to get away from governmental authorities entirely.

Computational currencies may also enable the super wealthy to withdraw from the nation-state system altogether, and enable the formation of stateless corporations that accept payments only in cryptocurrency, and whose home domicile is no country at all.

Sensing the magnitude of the threats it faces, one capacity that the state is developing with great focus is the ability to conduct the surveillance of its own citizens and visitors. This, too, will drive those with sufficient means to get away in the effort to regain their privacy. Thus, as the economy undergoes its relentless shift toward post-industrial digitalization, the nation-state itself is at risk of being shoved into irrelevance.

Geopolitics and its relationship with the modern corporation is rich with irony, as we see with Qualcomm:

'Qualcomm is an American technology firm that does 65% of its business in China, booked most of its profits in 2017 in Singapore, and pays little taxes in the US.

Nevertheless, it successfully lobbied the Trump administration to block a hostile takeover on the grounds that its independence was vital to ensure American strategic supremacy.'

The Economist
March 24, 2018

30

SUMMARY OF WORLD SHIFT
From Industrial to Digital

Billions of us now live in a consumerist, urbanized society of information excess that is entirely unlike anything that came before, the culture of industrial economy that created the modern world. Industrialization has reached in the present moment the very pinnacle of its remarkable development through the constant process of refinement and improvement in the highly competitive marketplace.

But now, almost entirely as a result of its own successes, the industrial economic process that created modernity is reaching the end of its amazing two hundred year run, bringing us to the edge of history's fourth monumental economic shift.

During prehistory, humanity transitioned from no-fire to fire, from the life of hunting and nomadism to agriculture, and in recent history from agriculture to industry. When industry was born, the concept of 'modernity' was also invented to describe a world culture that was exploring ideas and concepts at a furious rate, not sure where it was going but certain that the social and governmental structures of the agricultural past no longer served. New movements in art, architecture, music, dance, and literature sought to convey evolving ideas about our evolving experiences and expectations.

But along with these stunning new forms of expression, the modern world also brought new forms of violence, wars vastly more deadly and destructive than anything ever experienced. It was slaughter on the unprecedented scale of millions of casualties, cruelty spread across entire continents, followed then by post-war fears of nuclear annihilation with which we have lived for more than half a century.

Modernism has thus meant unparalleled material progress along side global-scale conflict, fabulous new wealth together with deep and enduring poverty and existential fear, a society in which billions enjoy lives of relative ease and abundance while other less fortunate billions suffer grinding poverty and deep insecurity, unable to meet basic needs for safety, food, water, decent habitat, or a future for their children. These profound disparities between rich and poor are stark, painful, and growing, and also a product of modern life. Will they also characterize the next economy?

For now we shift from industry to the digital economy, along with what else we don't yet know, all this occurring not because industrialism failed, but rather because it has succeeded so magnificently, and in so doing it created tools and techniques and problems that in aggregate are bringing about its own successor.

While the very concept of modernity was invented to provide a name for the pervasive impact that industrialism was having throughout economy and society, across all arts and sciences and in values and expectations, then what concepts will characterize the digital economy and the creative lifestyle?

Change like this, change at the scale of the global economy, does not occur because anyone decides that it ought to, nor according to any plan or intention. It happens because it expresses the aggregate of millions and billions of individual choices and actions, which become the whole of economic activity, a coalescing of the micro into macro ways of living that lead to the emergence of the overall patterns.

Now that the massive process of macro change is bringing us the world's fourth economic revolution with the rise of the digital economy, we can be sure that the world which our children and grandchildren will inhabit will be fundamentally different from ours. But we wonder, and we worry, Do we have the insight and foresight to prepare them for the new patterns, the new challenges, and the new opportunities?

'We are here for problem solving, not to get over into some universe with no problems of any kind. No, the better you are at problem solving, the worse the problems you're going to get. We are here for that. That is our function.'

Buckminster Fuller

31

ANTI SHIFT
From Nostalgia to Limitless Possibility

When change occurs in the basic structures and rules of the economy and society as it is today, this can have a liberating effect for those who are inspired to try something different, or who have been waiting for the opportunity to create something new. The elimination of limits frees those who experience renewed openness as the time for new possibilities, a time to discover new ideas and opportunities that were not so long ago inconceivable. They emerge to find their voices as promoters, advocates, creators, and entrepreneurs.

For others, however, the changing present era is unpleasant and frightening, and many lack confidence in our ability to successfully cope with the future and its large, intimidating, and ever-growing challenges. They feel we have lost control, and lost our way.

Thus, during times of rapid change we observe the emergence of opposing social forces. Promoters of change proclaim a shift, perhaps even a cultural revolution, a new day. Conversely, those who are frightened perceive all of this as regression and demise, and they may retreat inwardly or lash out violently. They may also promote counter-revolution in the determination to stop change from occurring.

Capitalizing on the pain of what has been lost, nationalist and xenophobic politicians arise, leading to extreme polarization of left from right, demonization, demagoguery, and the battle of progressive against conservative. The capacity for productive dialog and the willingness to seek middle ground and accept compromise are lost in ideological partisanship. With the fragmentation of micro-segmented media, every idea and ideology finds a dedicated channel and becomes an echo chamber of true and righteous belief, thereby widening the divide. Contrasting and indeed conflicting models and interpretations of reality bedevil ethics, economics, culture, education, religion, and government. Every aspect of society is dragged into partisanship.

For everyone, no matter what their view or expectation, the experience of uncertainty, vulnerability, and fear all increase, and thus stress increases as well. The desire that the future should be like the past lingers, and lamenting change, many yearn for the 'good old days,' and wish that life could return to the way it used to be. Under the spell of nostalgia's selective amnesia, the old days feel stable, comfortable, better, but perhaps that's because we've forgotten the bad parts.

And this of course is our situation today, revolution and counter-revolution existing side by side. But can it be resolved? Does shift or anti-shift prevail, or does extreme polarization foretell complete collapse?

Nostalgia is not a strategy, and no leader can succeed in making a nation or an organization great when the reference point that defines greatness is based on regression and blame, and when the underlying goal is reversion to an illusory and divisive past. What's needed is precisely the opposite. Anyway, the momentum of change that we have explored here throughout Part 1 suggests that whether they really were good or not, the old days are gone and nothing can bring them back.

Instead of nostalgia, it's the capacity to engage in understanding and mastering change that's essential, the mindset of curiosity and learning and inquiry, of exploration and confidence that we can indeed meet the new and as yet unknown challenges, we can create material value as well as cultural enrichment.

And what arises from this determination is the awareness that limits are indeed disappearing, and what replaces them is unlimited potential. This mindset requires that we expect change, prepare for change, and engage in learning about the emerging world, and then especially in creating positive change to steer its transformation.

'Rapid transformation destroys old coping mechanisms, old safety nets, while it creates a new set of demands, before new coping mechanisms are developed.'

Karl Polanyi
The Great Transformation

32

WORLD SHIFT MAKERS

The End of Industrialism

In the pre-industrial year of 1700 the most powerful nation in the European world was Spain, it's enormous wealth derived from mountains of gold and silver torn from its New World colonies, the practice of extractive *Colonial Capitalism*. One-hundred-thirty million Native Americans perished under Spanish rule, the worst genocide in history, but the riches were squandered in trivialities and the failed conquest of Great Britain, which ended with the sinking of the great Spanish Armada.

In 1800 the world's most powerful nation was France, which had thrown off its monarchy in favor of a republic, and which had found in Napoleon the most capable European general of his generation, or perhaps any generation since Alexander. Napoleon's triumphant armies subdued Europe for two decades and the wealth flowed back to Paris, until he met his match at Waterloo in 1815. It's said that during that last great battle Napoleon watched the British army maneuvers from a nearby hillside in admiration. 'They're learning!' he cried. They learned well, won the battle and the also war, and so Napoleon's reign of *Militaristic Capitalism* came to an abrupt end.

By 1900 the world's leading power was Great Britain, as Queen Victoria surveyed from London the largest mass of humanity and the greatest expanse of territory ever assembled into one empire. Britain's *Mercantilist Capitalism* enriched Londoners but impoverished the unfortunates in the colonies. A heavy blow to the empire was inflicted by World War I, and the fatal blow twenty-five years later with World War II; the empire was disbanded, leaving a small but proud island nation with rich memories of former glory.

A century later in 2000 *Industrial Capitalism* had carried the US to the world's economic and military pinnacle, but then greatness began slipping away as trillions of dollars were squandered in the failed attempt to remake the Middle East, followed by the debt-induced 2008 collapse, and capped off by the election of Donald Trump in 2016 based on campaign promises to restore America to its former greatness.

Which nation will dominate in 2100? Will it be China? That's unlikely, given the combination of its own toxic debt bomb and a demographic imbalance that will arise by mid-century, at which point China will likely follow Japan's path, a booming elderly population and economic malaise.

Perhaps instead it will a new nation, one that we don't know today. It could be *Blockchainistan*, a haven founded to escape the reach of national laws and currencies. Perhaps it will be *Automania* or *Robotopia*, owned and run by silicon intelligence rather than biological. If Kurzweil is correct and the robot singularity arrives by 2045, then by 2100 robots should be fully in control. It could also be the *United Republics of Outer Space*.

These are fanciful ideas, but not implausible. The point, of course, is that we often assume that the way things are now is how they will remain, which is certainly a false confidence. Change is the norm, the Big Shift has arrived, and so with the immanence of change in mind let's now step back and reflect on some of the key findings from Part 1.

- *Climate Shift* is already changing our lives and could enormously worsen if more food growing regions turn to deserts and if the glaciers melt and flood the urbanized coasts, casting billions into homelessness.
- *Robot Shift* is here en masse, 50,000 of them already laboring at Amazon.com alone, and more arriving daily. If the forecasts are correct then their sheer numbers will dwarf the human labor force within a decade, and if the forecast robot singularity is correct, then by mid-century the ratio of human intelligence to robot intelligence will shift irreversibly in the favor of the robots, and no one knows what happens then. (That's why it's a 'singularity,' because all the known rules break down at that point.)

'We are in that strange interregnum when the old order has collapsed and the new order is not yet born.

… A new global economic order is taking shape, but it is still confined within the brittle carapace of the old, with all of the outmoded, wasteful, oil-dependent, sprawling, unsustainable ways of life that went along with it.

… But the rise of a new social and economic order is a double-edged sword. It unleashes incredible energies, pointing the way toward new paths for unprecedented growth and prosperity, but it also causes tremendous hardships and inequality along the way.'

Richard Florida
The Rise of the Creative Class, Revisited

Continues on the next page

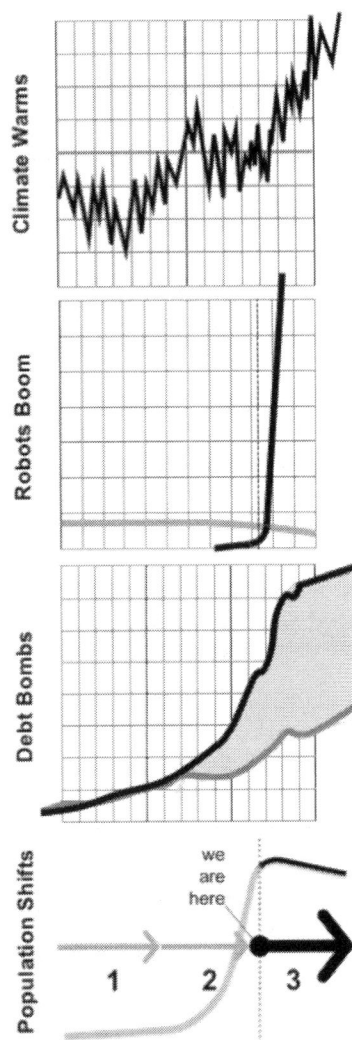

Four Drivers of the Big Shift

- Urbanization is driving the *population shift*, from an explosion to an implosion, but since the success of the industrial economy depended on an ever-expanding pool of laborer-consumers, implosion portends the demise of industrial consumerism, while the booming population of the aged will severely stress national health care systems and budgets.

- But maybe that doesn't really matter, because *debt shift bomb* and the financialization of the economy tell us that we're already living in a post-industrial system anyway. In the discussion about blockchains (see Section 21), I mentioned that Wall Street is being displaced by new forms of capital raising, but as you now understand that's merely pocket change compared to the trillions of dollars of debt and trading that Wall Street is handling now. Capital is reproducing capital, enriching the wealthy but creating stress for everyone else. Today the combined wealth of the world's 2200 billionaires is $9 trillion, greater than the wealth of the poorest 3.7 *billion* people combined (half the world's population). Each billionaire is thus worth the equivalent of about 1.6 million of the much less fortunate, showing is that the system is nicely enriching some, but definitely at the expense of many.

And so as I mentioned on the first page of the book, it's chaos out there. As I also mentioned, if one or a few of the key factors that shape a society and its economy are undergoing fundamental change then we naturally expect some impact on the overall structure of the economy. If many of the essentials change then we know something big is up.

> *But as all the factors are now experiencing fundamental change, then there is simply no escaping the fact that the entire system absolutely must change.*

This is the Big Shift, nothing short of the revolutionary transformation of society, the shift from industrialism to whatever comes next.

The idea that the next will be the digital economy is based on the total takeover that digital technology is *already* imposing across today's entire global economy, not only by robots but also genetic engineering, big data, VR and AR, artificial intelligence, and of course in the financialization of the whole shebang, all expressions of and dependent upon digitalization.

Looking back, then, we see that industrialization and cities grew together as science expanded, technology advanced, education improved, and then modern life came into being, an invention and by-product of the amazing industrial economic system. And now due to the brilliant successes of industrialism, a new and different economy is emerging, not by plan or design, but because incremental step by incremental step we have found our way into the digital revolution. And now, due to the fast cycles of positive feedback, technology gets better and better, enabling still more progress in technology, a process that appears to have no end-point.

> *This process of accelerating positive feedback is how the digital economy is bringing itself into being.*

It would require thousands of pages of detailed analysis to fully grasp all the important things that are happening (see the References section for a sampling), but even then the most important parts of the story could still not be told, *because they have not yet occurred.* We have thus arrived at a situation in which the uncertainties of the future overwhelm the certainties of present and past.

And as we experience these forces all acting at once, the consequence is an economic revolution that must inevitably lead to social transformation. Already we see rising fear and anger as people experience change but don't know what to make of it, and don't like the uncertainty it brings. Authoritarian and nationalist demagogues and media manufacture outrage to exploit these fears and disruptions, to incite still more fear and anger, and to raise their ratings.

In this dense and confusing situation we wish to understand the patterns that will help us to make sense of it all, and also to identify the pathways forward that will be positive and productive. These we will consider next in Parts 2 and 3.

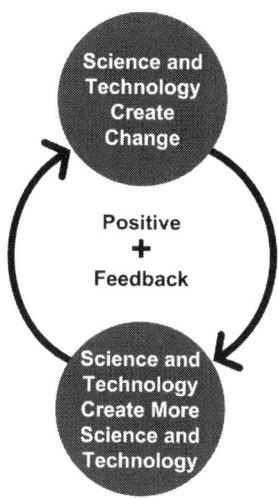

'Most long-range forecasts of what is technically feasible in future time periods dramatically underestimate the power of future developments. The 20th century was gradually speeding up to today's rate of progress; its achievements, therefore, were equivalent to about 20 years of progress at the rate in 2000. We'll make another 20 years of progress in just 14 years (by 2014), and then do the same again in only 7 years. So we won't experience one hundred years of technical advances in the 21st century; we will witness on the order of 20,000 years of progress (as measured by today's rate of progress).'

Ray Kurzweil
The Singularity Is Near

PART 2

MINDSET SHIFT

New Patterns for a New Economy

Given all the shifts described in Part 1, the changing dynamics of technology, manufacturing, population, resources, and climate, and the digital economy that is emerging as the confluence of all of these forces of change, how are we going to prepare ourselves, how are we going to adapt, and how will we succeed within its still-developing constraints and possibilities?

This is first of all a challenge of *mindset*, a challenge to understand the fundamental and important patterns that are shaping the future. Once we grasp the essential patterns we then have to adjust our mental models and expectations to fit the new realities.

Here in Part 2 we examine the essential patterns and the shifts of mind that will enable us to understand, to cope, and to succeed. We thus focus on understanding the key characteristics of new economy, and the patterns and processes of change itself.

We begin by looking at a factor that so many of the shifts have in common, the pattern of exponential change.

MINDSET SHIFT

NEXT ECONOMY ▶ **33**

EXPONENTIAL SHIFT
From Gently Slow to Wicked Fast

Many of us visualize change in the form of a gently ascending line. Its gracious slope shows how things are gradually becoming different from the past. Change, this line tells us, is quite manageable.

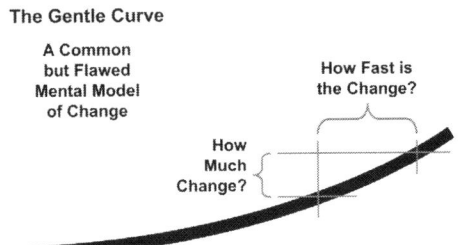

The Gentle Curve

A Common but Flawed Mental Model of Change

How Fast is the Change?

How Much Change?

The first essential pattern that we must grasp is that this is a quite poor representation of today's changes, because today they're neither slow nor linear. They don't arrive at a measured pace, a step at a time, evenly. Change today is driven by vicious positive feedback loops, making it non-linear, exponential, and wicked. The real meaning of exponential, however, is difficult for most of us to grasp. Over the millions of years of evolution there haven't been many exponential phenomena in our world, so we not only fail to recognize them, we also fail to appreciate how enormous their impacts are likely to be.

But when you grasp how life-changing they are, and as you look at the graphs on the facing page, the situation becomes clear, and quite frightening. Indeed, in the insightful words of Ford executive Jim Farley (and others), 'If you're not scared, you're not paying attention.' Or in simpler and more modern language, 'OMG!'

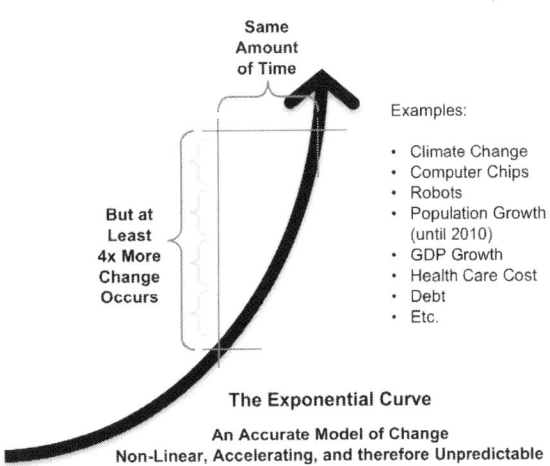

Same Amount of Time

But at Least 4x More Change Occurs

Examples:

- Climate Change
- Computer Chips
- Robots
- Population Growth (until 2010)
- GDP Growth
- Health Care Cost
- Debt
- Etc.

The Exponential Curve

An Accurate Model of Change
Non-Linear, Accelerating, and therefore Unpredictable

I tried to explain this recently to a friend as we were discussing climate change. He said, 'It took 200 years to raise the CO_2 level to what it is now, so I figure we have another 200 years before we really need to worry about it.' That may be have been true in a linear world, but it's not true not in our world. Change is accelerating, and we don't have 200 years. We may not even have 20.

All the exponential graphs in Part 1 tell essentially the same story: change is accelerating, and the Big Shift to the next economy isn't linear. It's coming faster and faster.

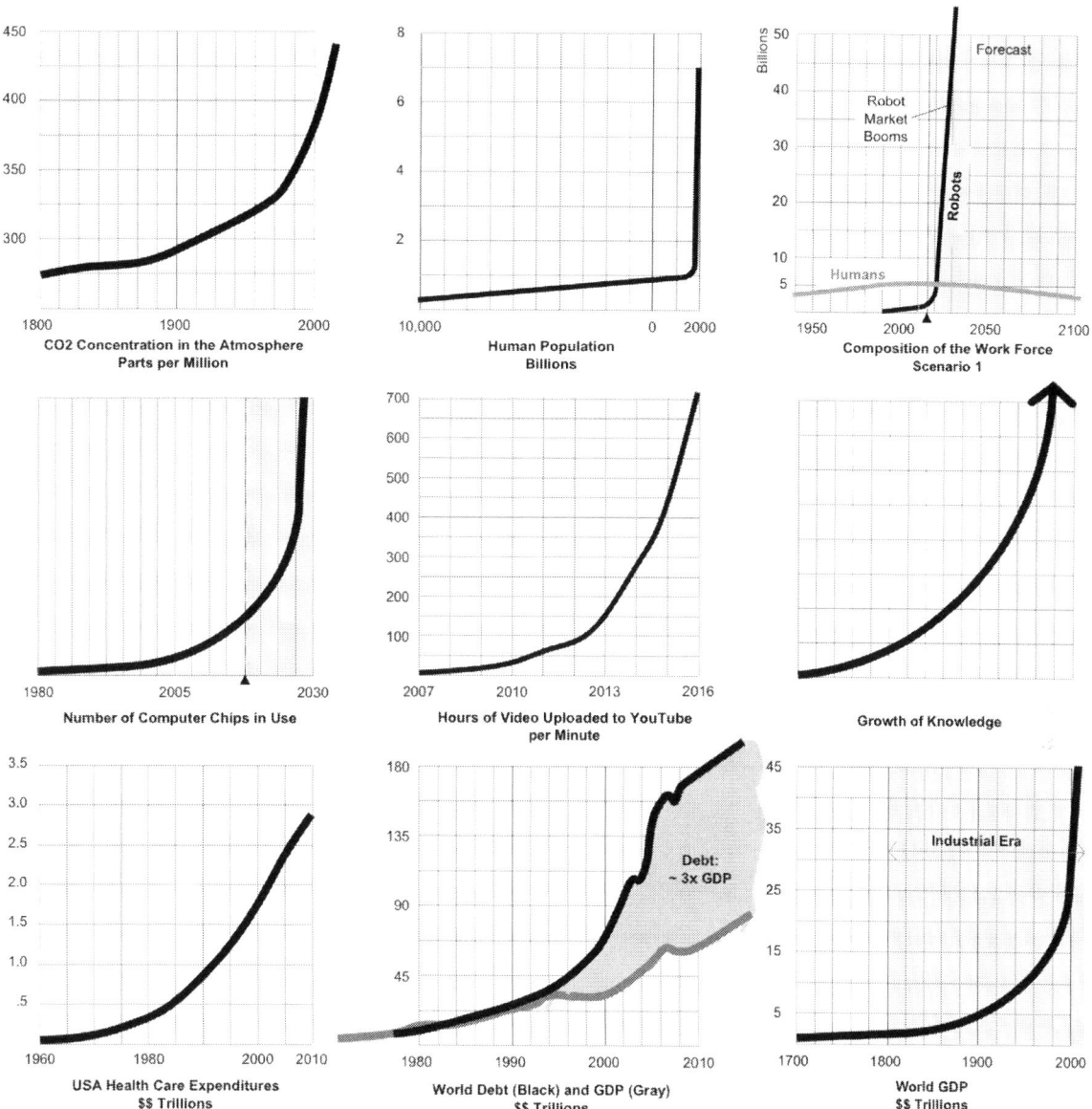

CO2 Concentration in the Atmosphere
Parts per Million

Human Population
Billions

Composition of the Work Force
Scenario 1

Number of Computer Chips in Use

Hours of Video Uploaded to YouTube
per Minute

Growth of Knowledge

USA Health Care Expenditures
$$ Trillions

World Debt (Black) and GDP (Gray)
$$ Trillions

World GDP
$$ Trillions

9 Exponential Trends
'If you're not scared, you're not paying attention.'

34

DIGITALIZATION SHIFT
From Industrial to Digital

Having worked our way through the discussion of all those exponential changes that all point to the demise of industrialism, what can we now say with confidence about the next economy?

For one thing, we can obviously reflect on the arrival of massive digitalization. Consider, for example, that as recently as a decade or two ago a bank was a financial services firm, a retailer was a seller of goods, and a car company was in the transportation business. Today that's no longer true. Now they're *all* technology companies, and if their leaders have ignored or resisted this important transition then they're probably no longer in business, or will soon be gone.

Technology has transformed all products into digital products, and all markets into digital markets. Its continuing colonization of the world economy thus requires that every firm recognize that the digital domain is an essential core element of its business model no matter what else it's doing or making or selling. This is the digitally-enabled economy that has superseded the industrial one, and with the arrival of the robots it's only more digital for as far as the eye can see.

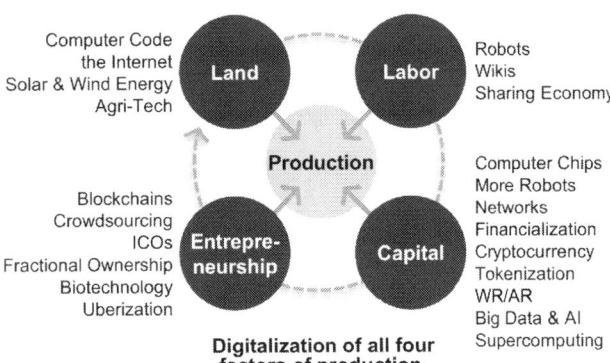

Digitalization of all four factors of production.

The figure to the left describes this new reality by showing how each element of the classical economic model has transitioned to a digital form over the last few decades. Land and climate are still land and climate, but all else is or soon will be substantially or totally digitized. And although today we're apparently living during the transition period between industrial and digital, if you magically removed the digital from the present economy you'd create nearly instant collapse, and because we're so entirely dependent upon it this provides us with a glimpse of what's coming. This is in fact one of the key indications that the digital economy is next, because nothing else comes even close to the importance of the digital world as an overall economic organizing principle.

There are two dimensions to our dependency on digital. First is the *digital infrastructure*, the internet and mobile phones and satellites and GPS and apps and servers and all that, and the chips that run the whole show. They're the means through which businesses and the economy as a whole now function, how nearly all transactions are negotiated, how commerce is managed, how payments are transmitted and tracked.

The other dimension is the content, the *information content* that all this infrastructure is sending around for us, zipping it from device to device so instantaneously and apparently effortlessly. The gazillions of YouTube videos, Twitter feeds, Instagrams and VPNs and wikis and emails and blockchains, Google searches and Amazon digital catalogs.

The combination of digital infrastructure and content has radically reshaped the economy during the last 25 years, disrupting industry after industry. Many jobs that were common in 1990 don't exist today, while entirely new ones have taken their place. The turnover among companies has been equally swift, and it's accelerating as corporate lifespans shrink due to the intensity of competition and the arrival new digital competitors, Uber, Netflix, Google, and Amazon being obvious examples.

In addition to its direct economic impact, all this content also creates an entirely new social infrastructure, a fundamental change in the way society communicates with itself and identifies itself. In today's world you're hardly real if you don't have a web site or a Facebook page.

And because information is distributed so effortlessly now, it's fundamentally changing how organizations function. Now the networks matter more than the hierarchies, decision making is different, and the ways that we create and use knowledge are also quite different. We will examine all these themes in the following sections and in Part 3 as we compose a more complete picture of the emerging digital economy.

Computer code and the **internet** are new forms of virtual 'land,' resource infrastructure upon which we have new means to create wealth.

Wikis are digital platforms for the collaborative creation and sharing of knowledge content. They function outside of the traditional business environment, as the objective isn't profit, but they compete with and often out-compete old business models, like encyclopedias.

The **Sharing Economy** describes new ways for assets to be owned, used, and monetized.

Tokenization means creating a digital record of ownership using blockchains to manage and attest to the disposition of assets.

Uberization refers to digital businesses that integrate mobile technology, new forms of asset management, and the sharing economy into new and disruptive business models.

35

CREATIVE SHIFT
From Jobs to Visions

NEXT ECONOMY

It is the entrepreneurs who organize all the other factors to create new enterprises. There is the idea for the business, the capital to make it run, the machines and the people, the investors and business partners and advisors, and of course the customers. Successfully creating a business a century ago or today requires above all else one exceptional quality, which is creativity. That the entrepreneur does this in pursuit of commercial opportunity and perhaps personal wealth is secondary to the profound act of creation that is embodied in any successful new venture.

The creative entrepreneurs of the past invented industrialism and founded companies that still span the globe, and today's have equally compelling visions and sometimes amazing accomplishments.

And so it will be tomorrow.

And thus the third major pattern to consider after exponential shift and new technologies in the next economy is the role of creativity. Some have even suggested that we're transitioning into a *creative economy* because they believe that creativity itself will be the defining factor of the future, and there's plenty of evidence to suggest that this may be true. Certainly the highly creative digital entrepreneurs will have enormous impact, and so for that matter will the creators of new financial instruments.

And so also will the graphic designers, the film makers, the game designers, fashion designers, musicians, architects and urban designers and scientists. All their roles will be central, and so will their collaborations with one another, so much so that it's quite reasonable to suggest that creativity will indeed be the essential defining characteristic of the next economy. We already use social media enabling each of us to create a unique online identity, and as we extend this logic it's not at all a stretch to suggest that the next economy will be all about creating lives and lifestyles. Especially if

'The rise of the Creative Economy is drawing the spheres of innovation (technological creativity), business (economic creativity), and culture (artistic and cultural creativity) into one another, in more intimate and more powerful combinations than ever.'

Richard Florida
The Rise of the Creative Class, Revisited

the robots are doing all the nasty, yucky work.

Customized products and services, new concepts and memes, designer clothing and designer jeans and genes are all part of our near term future.

In Part 3 we'll take up the notion of creativity and its close partner innovation, as these are two of the most important skills for tomorrow, but for our purposes here, where the overall topic is the new mindset, it's clear that the creative mindset will be absolutely essential regardless of the form that the future economy takes. Increasing emphasis on creativity will have major impacts throughout education, and it will also change how people think about employment.

Whereas in the past it was common for people to think about getting an education as the means to getting 'a job,' more and more we will see a shift in the purpose of education. We will instead seek more learning not because we want to become eligible to be employed by someone else, but rather to gain the knowledge necessary to turn our creative passions and interests into satisfying and successful ventures and lifestyles. This is the entrepreneurial explosion that we discussed in Part 1 enabled by the changing role of entrepreneurial finance through crowdsourcing and the ICO.

Robots may or may not turn out to be usefully creative, but there will always be vitally important roles for creative people with the skills, the drive, and the mindset to change the world through their ideas, and through their entrepreneurial visions and aspirations.

'Knowledge is actually what gives imagination its power, what makes creativity possible. It's because we know something about how events are connected in the world that we can imagine altering those connections and creating new ones. It's because we know about this world that we can create possible worlds.'

Alison Gopnik
The Philosophical Baby

36

METAPHOR SHIFT
From Horsepower to Exabytes

1955 was the first year in which the Fortune 500 list was published. In that year the largest American companies by revenue were the industrial giants GM, Exxon, US Steel, GE, and Esmark (a meat packing firm).

In 2017 the largest US firms were Wal-Mart, Berkshire Hathaway, Apple, Exxon-Mobil, and McKesson, which gives us an idea just how much the economy has evolved. A retailer and a consumer conglomerate replaced an auto maker and an oil company at one and two, a technology company replaced a steel maker at three, and a health care company replaced a meat packing company at five, besides which the 2017 top 5 earned 50 times more in combined revenue.

1955		2017	
General Motors	10	Walmart	486
Exxon	6	Berkshire Hathaway	223
US Steel	4	Apple	215
General Electric	3	Exxon	205
Esmark	3	McKesson	192
	26		1,321

Fortune 500, USA
Revenue, Billions of Dollars

During the next twenty years, technology's share of economic activity will continue to increase as we experience still more waves of technology exploding into use, and so as we think ahead and wonder what companies will be at the top of the list in 2025, it's obvious that industrial giants won't be the biggest firms, but that the digitally-enabled 'internet of things' universe will become even more dominant.

iPhones, responsive web sites, and auto-correcting software are among the tools we use today to take advantage of the deeper hidden world of technology; tomorrow's technologies will be embedded into our clothing and jewelry, tattooed directly to our skin or inserted just below it, built right into our artificial joints, and printed into machine-made organs. Computers will disappear as devices and instead become embedded into everything, so we won't 'use' computers, we'll live within 'digital environments.'

For this we will require new language. Consider, for example, that during the agricultural era the dominant technologies were considered to be the 'workhorses' of the economy, while during the industrial era we called them the 'engines' that 'drove' the economy. We measured the power of machines in terms of the previous era's benchmark – horses – thus giving us the measures of a car's power as 'horsepower.' In the current economy one of the most coveted of jobs is that of the 'software engineer,' but what do engines have to do with coding software? Essentially nothing, but the language pattern remains with us, a vestige of the prior age.

As we have not adjusted our language, nor have we adjusted our ways of working and thinking. Many of our concepts are flawed, no longer fitting the reality of the emerging economic system we are in the process of creating.

While today's computer chips are central to nearly all economic activity, we still lack common language metaphors to adequately describe the digital technology-enabled economy's creative force, and the models to manage it. It's not horses or engines, it's processing speed and storage capacity measured as MIPS and flops, and terabytes, petabytes, and exabytes, software code by the millions and billions of lines, and transmission speeds by clockspeed in gigahertz.

None of these terms have made it into the popular lexicon, as they're considerably more abstract than the horses and cars that used to be such vivid physical presences in our lives, livelihoods, and mental images. But now that we're shifting to a digital economy we'll shift to new metaphors as well.

Hence, the new metaphors are coming, along with the new companies that will dominate future of technology and commerce, and also perhaps to fill our children's imaginations with ideas of what may soon become possible.

'Virtually all of the economic models taught in economics classes and used by the Federal Reserve Board to set monetary policy, by government agencies to set economic policy, and by economic forecasters of all kinds are fundamentally flawed in their view of long-term trends.

That's because they're based on the linear view of history (the assumption that the pace of change will continue at the current rate) rather than the historically based exponential view.

The reason these linear models appear to work for a while is the same reason most people adopt the linear view in the first place: exponential trends appear to be linear when viewed and experienced for a brief period of time, particularly in the early stages. But once the knee of the curve is achieved and the exponential growth explodes, the linear models break down.'

Raw Kurzweil
The Singularity Is Near

37

EXPECTATION SHIFT
From Static to Dynamic

NEXT ECONOMY

In 1899 the Commissioner of the US Patent and Trademark Office suggested that the office should be closed down since 'everything that can be invented has been invented.' His idea reflected a common belief at the time, that society had reached a point of near perfection. A few modest inventions did however emerge later, including the auto, the airplane, the rocket, satellites, iPhones, and so on. In fact the entire the modern world came after.

How could he have gotten it ridiculously and humorously and entirely wrong to think that the world of 1899 was the end of creativity, invention, innovation or change, when it was just the beginning?

Obviously he made a gigantic mental error, mistaking a momentary present for a trend, thinking it was the perfection of one era when it was really the pre-dawn of the next one.

Others have made the same mistake. In 1989 Francis Fukuyama rose to prominence when he published the book *The End of History* in which he suggested that the collapse of the Soviet Union marked the ultimate triumph of the western, democratic, capitalist model of society. He was also entirely wrong, as he would admit some years later, embarrassed no doubt by the abundance of important historical events that subsequently occurred.

In 2006 Allan Greenspan understood that the economy had reached a point of permanent balance from which only good outcomes would result. The major recession which followed very soon thereafter exposed his expectations as fundamentally unfounded, and his imagination as somewhat limited.

These predictions have three important things in common, in addition to being entirely erroneous. First, of course, they reflected a deep misunderstanding of their times. Second, they revealed a flawed thinking process, in which preference and self-satisfaction displaced rigor and the

'This crisis has turned out to be much broader than anything I could have imagined.'

Alan Greenspan
October 22, 2008

84

intellectual discipline that might have revealed more useful insights.

Third is that they reflected the profoundly erroneous expectation that capitalist economic system can ever achieve a point of stability, or stasis, following which things will stay the same for any extended period of time.

This is particularly relevant not because a few people who should have known better had unfounded expectations and made silly comments, but because this mental error is so common. People in all societies and across all eras make the same mistake, expecting that the way things are now is how they are destined to remain, when the opposite is true.

Capitalism is a system that is compelled to make change in ways that are inherently unpredictable because it always seeks opportunity in an inherently dynamic marketplace.

The 31 shifts described in Part 1 tell the story of the capitalist process as a relentless creator of change, the process through which agriculture created industry and industry is now creating its successor economy. These same shifts also tell us that change is now arriving even faster and more furiously than we've ever experienced, and to expect anything other than more change is probably foolish.

What's needed instead is readiness for change and a mindset ready to abandon stasis, the realization that our entire situation is fundamentally dynamic, and that no matter how bad or good it is now it's inevitably going to change. The enduring success strategy is therefore to expect change, prepare for it, and especially to be the creator of change.

(Note that to be the creator of change means to be an innovator, which will examine in detail in Part 3.)

General Electric, created by merger by Thomas Edison in 1892, has been included in the Dow Jones Industrial Average since 1896, the year the index was created. Until June 26, 2018, that is, when it was kicked out of the Dow because of its declining performance.

Change is indeed relentless.

In the words of *The Economist*, 'Mismanagement and a failure to move with the times have turned the erstwhile icon of innovation into a disorganized, debt-laden mess. GE's shares have plunged to below a quarter of their peak value in 2000.'

The Economist
June 30, 2018

38

MEASUREMENT SHIFT
From GDP to Well-Being

Prior to industrialization, the means and measures by which society allocated resources were organized around land and its productive capacity, as it was deeply understood through hard experience that the land requires care or it will degrade. Social obligations were likewise accepted, so many resources were shared as 'common wealth,' and even private property was thought of somewhat differently. Thus, as an organizing paradigm or model, industrialism's short history of only 200 years was preceded by millennia of a much different understanding of the role of resources in society.

Once the industrial economic model took hold, its orientation around capital as the organizing force created the expectation that growth is a constant necessity, and that all forms of resources are commodities to be fed into the industrial process. This then led to the obsession with its measurement as GDP, gross domestic product, the statistical sum of all economic activity.

While we often mistakenly assume that people always thought this way, in fact the GDP-centric view focused on private capital was invented only in 1934. The concept never existed before industrialism, and reflects industrialism's inherent organizing structure in service to private capital and its growth.

GDP is exclusively quantitative, and does not consider 'better' or 'worse,' only 'more' or 'less.' More coal burned is thus an economic 'good,' as is more money spent on health care for lung disease caused by coal's air pollution. The flaws in this logic are obvious when destruction of the environment and health sacrificed for industrial purposes is counted as 'good.'

The reason for this error of thought is that GDP makes a distinction between private capital and private goods that are measurable and therefore measured, and public capital and public goods whose value is not so easily determined.

To sustain growth, production and consumption must continually increase, and so industrial economics silently assumes that more resources will become available to be consumed, and that a place will be found for all the resulting waste. On a finite planet that is already over-consuming these assumptions are now exposed as false, and they'll certainly have to be revised as we transition to the digital economy.

In the digital economy economists will learn to model and to factor into their assessments of economic health not only to *how much* stuff is consumed and wasted and how much private capital has grown thereby, but factors including *quality of production* and *quality of life*, *well being*, and the health of the environment, all of which are presently excluded from the GDP calculation.

And as we learn to ask and to measure how good or poor is quality of life, how fair or unfair is access to food, water, and shelter, and what are the implications of patterns of use and consumption for the future, we will embed a shared responsibility back into the economy, and we will create new organizing metrics to reflect this more comprehensive and holistic viewpoint.

We measure what we value, and then we tend to value what we measure, but only because it's measured. We mistake test scores and grades for learning because we can measure test results but not knowledge or wisdom, and we have mistakenly equated GDP with the creation of value because it counts the countable value of private capital while perversely considering public good and public capital as disposable means. A shift in how we measure economic value creation is necessarily on its way.

•••

These, then, are the key elements of the next economy, exponential change, digitalization, creativity, shifting expectations, and new ways to measure what's important. Next we will consider the *new patterns* that explain the process of change itself, and which we are learning to recognize, understand, and manage.

'For several generations, economic growth as defined by GDP has been the dominant story, the logic of our culture. Most people alive today cannot remember a time when the performance of economies was not measured by GDP.

And the logic of GDP foresees no end to growth. Our collective performance can receive and A+ even if large numbers of people are out of work, a sense of community and purpose is disappearing, inequality is rising, resources are depleted, and nature is turned into parking lots. Endless growth on a finite planet simply does not add up.

Bad measures inevitably lead to bad results.'

Dirk Philipsen
The Little Big Number

NEW PATTERNS ▶ # 39

NEW PATTERN SHIFT
From Change to Positive Feedback

History reveals whatever we have learned with the benefit of hindsight, the flows of changes, shifts, new events and trends that altered previous ways of life.

Looking backwards we label these shifts to organize our understanding of the past. Hence, geologists describe history in the eras known as the Paleozoic (ancient life, from 540 million to 250 million years ago), Mesozoic (middle life, from 250 million years ago until 66 million years ago), and Cenozoic (recent life, from 66 million years ago until today). Chinese dynastic history begins with the Xia beginning about 4000 years ago, followed by the Shang and later the Zhou and later still the Han, Tang, and Song. Europe's eras include the Ancient World of the Mediterranean and its interactions across Mesopotamia, the Roman Empire and North Africa, the Medieval Era, the Renaissance, the Enlightenment, etc. Economic history writ large is marked by the great ages labeled the Stone Age, the Agricultural Age, and the Industrial Age.

The point for us of course is that these groupings help us to recognize broader patterns of change. They help us to understand what brought each era to its close, and what forces have most strongly catalyzed the shift from one era, age, or dynasty to the next.

Looking forward we'd like to do the same, and so our challenge is to invert our perspective to see the emerging patterns, to understand the future. The problem is of course the essential rub of all attempts at foresight, that the future cannot be predicted.

Changes across history did not occur because someone said they should. No king, emperor, president, prime minister, and surely no economist decided that the industrial economy should arise, none of them had the power to make it happen, nor to stop it. Instead, it occurred because many people decided in the moment whatever it was that made the most sense for themselves, their enterprises, their families, and so they made it happen step by step.

And this is how it's happening with the arrival of next economy as well. Its emergence is not according to a plan, but because of everything unplanned that's nevertheless happening – the growth of science, the explosion of technology, climate change, resource depletion, booming urbanism, peaking population, etc. etc., just as no one insisted that YouTube usage would explode, but it has too. The system, in other words, isn't under anyone's control; it moves forward of its own volition.

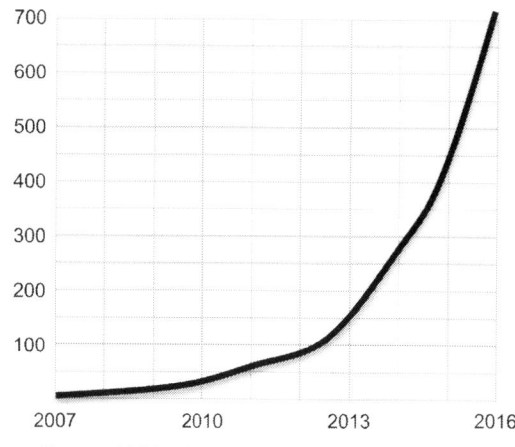

Hours of Video Uploaded to YouTube – per Minute

This cycle that drives change, the process by which science begets more science, knowledge begets more knowledge, change begets more change, is as we saw above known as positive feedback. It explains why change accelerates, as more begets still more, which induces more to occur faster. This is the essential dynamic that enabled industrial economics to grow and encompass nearly all economic activity worldwide, and it is the dynamic that is now pushing society beyond industrialism and on to its next organizing structure.

Thus, the one pattern that history reveals above all others is the constant unfolding of change. It's not stability and repetition we observe, but rather a continual flow of shifts and differences; it's not a story about things staying as they were, it's about how new knowledge and changing conditions define new challenges that evoke new responses. As these responses accumulate the entire structure of life, the economy, culture, values and attitudes, and expectations change as well, bringing us now to the Big Shift.

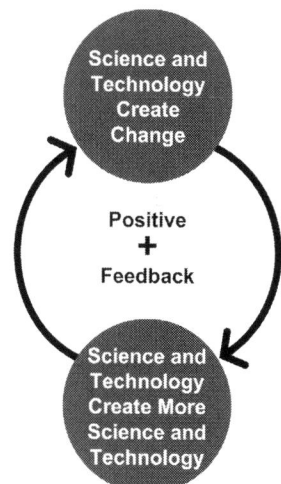

40

PARADIGM SHIFT
From Old Models to New

NEW PATTERNS

Science is the organized pursuit of new knowledge, meaning that scientists who work in any given field are constantly engaged in the search for knowledge about its inevitable unknowns. Their precise objective is to discover new knowledge and determine how it fits with the old data, concepts, theories, and models, all of which they use to organize their work. As scientists proceed they also inevitably uncover errors, discrepancies, unresolvable problems, and inconsistencies. Perhaps these anomalies had avoided notice before, or perhaps the tools and techniques previously employed had been unable to detect these more refined or granular distinctions.

In most fields, the anomalous data and discoveries are considered outliers because they do not fit existing theory, and since established scientific theories have adherents who believe them and defenders whose careers and even identities are tied to a particular model or worldview, the importance of anomalies is often discounted and their veracity may be disputed entirely.

Nevertheless, eventually and inevitably tools and techniques become more sophisticated, and finer measurements define new knowledge which calls into question underlying models and theories. Soon the entire field is forced to confront the dilemma that the new data and old models do not match; that is, old models and theories do not adequately explain the new data.

A difficult situation now arises as the question becomes, 'Which is right? Is it the new data or the old theories wherein the problem lies?'

If the new data are correct then new theory and models are needed to explain them, new organizing principles and concepts, as the old models are no longer adequate. For those attached to old models, however, the new data are held as unreliable, (as we see today, for example, with climate change denial).

At this point there exist two different and possibly conflicting theories to explain the base data, and the field divides for a time into opposing camps. Perhaps they are labeled the 'Newtonians' and the 'Einsteinians.'

Eventually someone, or a team, or individuals working independently and in parallel land upon an alternative explanation for the basic facts, and the new data are thus validated because the new theory or model better accounts for the data they have painstakingly gathered.

In the field of study known as 'philosophy of science' this process of significant change is referred to as a *paradigm shift*. This invaluable concept was developed by Thomas S. Kuhn, whose profoundly influential book 1962 *The Structure of Scientific Revolutions* explains how scientists think about their work and how science progresses. The book also led to a major shift in our understanding, for in it Kuhn demonstrated how scientific knowledge progresses through punctuated starts, leaps, or in Kuhn's terminology, from the lock-in of an old paradigm to the shift to a new one.

Kuhn described the often painful process through which a field transitions from universal acceptance of an old paradigm to sporadic and then eventually universal acceptance of a new one, a shift of thinking, of mindset, that creates a shift of work as scientists then begin collecting data in the context of the new theory and its models, and so the cycle continues.

The world was flat, and then it wasn't. The Earth was the center of universe, and then not. Newton's laws defined all physical reality, and then they didn't.

The relevance of this to our discussion of the Big Shift should be obvious; what *we're* going through is a paradigm shift, an economic one that requires us to grapple with and eventually accept new data and new models (a new mindset), and soon to adapt to life after industrialism, which also requires new skills. We also can use some help visualizing how this change occurs, as we will discover next.

'The parallel between political and scientific development should no longer be open to doubt. ... In increasing numbers individuals become increasingly estranged from political life. ... Society is divided into competing camps or parties, one seeking to defend the old institutional constellation, the others seeking to institute some new one.

Once that polarization has occurred, political recourse fails.'

Thomas S. Kuhn
The Structure of Scientific Revolutions

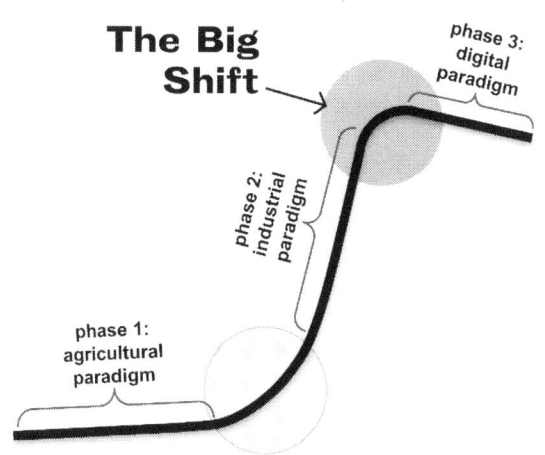

The Big Shift

phase 3: digital paradigm

phase 2: industrial paradigm

phase 1: agricultural paradigm

41

STAIRCASE SHIFT
From Smooth to Punctuated

NEW PATTERNS

As we discussed in Section 33, the slowing ascending curve is an erroneous model of how change is occurring today. Instead, it's much more accurate to represent change as an exponential curve, its steeply rising line suggesting that changes are coming very fast. We've used this very same curve to show how the population increased from 1800 to 2000, how the economy has grown along with it, how fossil fuel usage grew and then CO_2 as well, how technology has boomed, in particular because the exact same curve also shows Moore's Law, the inexorable increase in computing power. The exponential curve is clearly a key description of our world.

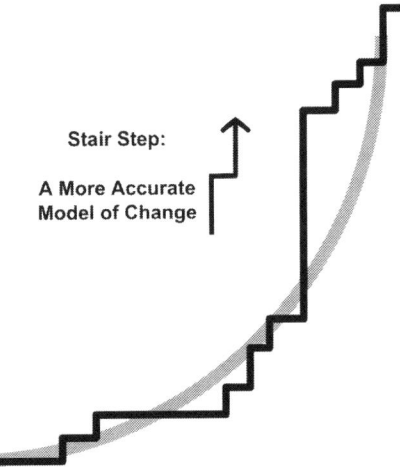

Stair Step:

A More Accurate Model of Change

But we can do even better, and now that I've introduced the concept of paradigm change we can visualize it. Change, it turns out, can best be understood not as a curve, but as a series leaps, or advances that look like the steps of a staircase. The overall process of change is thus revealed as periods of relative stability, whether for a short or long durations (shown by the horizontals), punctuated by instances of abrupt shifts in the trajectory, the steps up (or possibly down) to the new way.

The vertical marks the abrupt arrival of the new thing, whether it's an event such as war or peace, a technology such as a computer chip or a rocket, or a social change such as the right to vote or the New Deal. The vertical, of course, denotes the paradigm change itself.

Notice also how the staircase concept permits us to pinpoint the instance of paradigm change. It's the big leap, of course, signifying a major shift in how we live or what we believe, or both.

The same concept has been developed in the field of evolutionary biology, where scientists refer to this as 'punctuated equilibrium.' Periods of relative stability, equilibrium, are signified by the flat part of the line, but they are interrupted, or punctuated, by the sudden and unpredictable emergence of mutations as shown by the verticals. The key point is that the changes which disrupt any ecological status quo come not regularly and predictably, but intermittently and unpredictably. Each leap causes a new status quo to result, represented as the next flat step. This is a very helpful model for students of change, like us, because it alerts us to look for the shifts, and *not* to expect smoothness in the ebbs and flows of history.

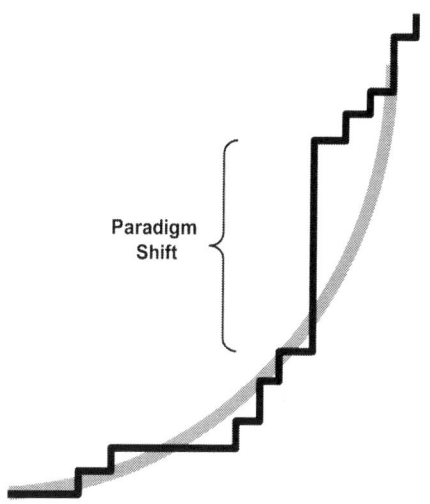

Paradigm Shift

This concept also causes us to wonder what leads to the punctuations, and the answer is twofold, one internal and the other external. *Internal* change in evolution is the mutation, the altered genetic structure that enables new behavior or causes debilitating deficiency. A mutation in the genes of the eye, for example, could result in significantly improved vision, or in blindness, but until a mutation is manifested in an offspring, its impact is unknowable.

External change that drives evolution is change to the environment, such as a change in climate (uh-oh), or a shift in the population, prey, predators, or the food chain.

The applications to our time are unmistakable. We are creating shifts in the gene pool now through genetic engineering, literally changing the vector of our own evolutionary path, and at the same time the power of industrialization is changing the external environment at a furious rate – the climate and the food chain, the air and water, all subject to massive human influence.

Today in fact we are 'all shift and no stasis,' and it's all happening all at once, step after upwards step we rise on the staircase of change, reminding us that the steep staircase is a quite accurate model of accelerating change, while the shallow one is an inaccurate and possibly dangerous preconception.

And as our understanding of how change is occurring is itself shifting, so too must our way of making decisions.

42

DECISION SHIFT
From Bias to Evidence

NEW PATTERNS

Managers often feel that their decisions are objective and rational, reached after taking into consideration all the pertinent facts. Psychologists and business scholars, however, have found otherwise. They've identified a long inventory of deficient modes of thinking that continue to be common, and which commonly cause lots of problems. The general category is called 'cognitive bias,' modes of thinking that routinely deceive us, and in so doing cause our decisions to go awry.

A bias is an assumption or expectation about the way the world works that's based not on evidence, but on habit, preference, or prejudice. Many biases are residual beliefs based on prior experiences, but no longer valid; the world has shifted but we've not grasped the change. Does that sound familiar?

It's the expectation that change is a gentle curve when in fact the universe has given us an exponential one. Here are seven other common biases that affect thinking and decision-making:

1. *Denial:* It's easy to ignore contradictory evidence and see only what we want to see. Did you ever hear someone say, 'I refuse to believe...?' or 'That can't be right...' (even though it is)? The more deeply a position is tied to an ideological commitment, the easier it is to fall into this trap.

2. *Just this morning:* Vivid, easily imaginable, and recent events are often weighted disproportionately in making decisions. Something that occurred this morning, even if it's insignificant, may exert disproportionate influence in the decision making process. 'Why just this morning I saw....'

3. *Justification:* Data are collected *after* an event serve to justify a decision, while contradictory evidence is often disregarded. If 'it *can't* be true' it is often ignored, at our peril.

4. *Escalation:* Previous decisions influence present decisions, as when we 'put good money after bad.' Unwillingness to walk away from bad outcomes leads us to keep investing more in the futile attempt to turn hopeless situations around. For example, having lost tens of thousands of soldiers in Vietnam, the U.S. president was unwilling to lose face and abandon the doomed war, and consequently lost tens of thousands more in addition to many times that in casualties among the Vietnamese. 'We've paid too high a price to back out now' leads to escalation.

   Often it's the next president (or CEO) who must unwind the disaster, because the original decision maker can never admit to the futility.

5. *Framing:* How a situation is presented affects decisions, and they can be easily if unconsciously framed to validate a given expectation or position. 'Of course you agree that ...' is a common framing error.

6. *Hindsight:* It's easy to construct a logical story to explain events in hindsight even though we really had no clue as to what was coming. Nassim Taleb explains in *The Black Swan* that, 'Past events will always look less random than they were.'

7. *Groupthink:* Decision making and advisory groups often prefer social cohesion and friendliness to serious debate on the merits of contentious issues. If you find yourself thinking, 'He's totally wrong about that but I don't want to say anything...' then you're probably engaging in groupthink.

The remedy for each of these cognition errors is to rigorously rely on *evidence*, which requires, of course, that we distinguish between evidence and preference, between assumptions and certified valid observations, between narrow opinion and actual possibility, between ideological prejudice and sound analysis. Effective decision making therefore requires clear thinking, relentless questioning, and determined discipline, all of which are essential in these times of rapid change.

In this effort we will benefit enormously from science.

43

SCIENCE SHIFT
From Old Knowledge to More

NEW PATTERNS

'Science knows no country, because knowledge belongs to humanity, and is the torch which illuminates the world'

Louis Pasteur

Most of the scientists who have ever lived throughout the entire history of humanity are still alive, and even more amazingly they're still doing science today. Each year the world's universities graduate even more, and so the oceans of knowledge that humanity has access to grows ever larger. Their work drives change and the acceleration of history, as their discoveries eventually call old scientific facts and models into question while creating new and better models, or paradigms, to replace them.

This process of paradigm shift is sometimes expressed through a quaint story about the first day of medical school. The college dean stands on stage before the assembled group of expectant doctors-to-be and welcomes them to the esteemed institution where they will be diligently working for the coming years to master the magnificent field of medicine.

'Welcome!' she proclaims grandly as she smiles warmly. 'During the next four years you'll work very hard, and you'll master a huge volume of valuable knowledge that our faculty is looking forward to sharing with you. Congratulations!'

But she continues with a frown. 'Unfortunately, however, about half of what you are about to learn is incorrect. In the coming years, science will disprove a significant number of the 'facts' that you are about to learn.'

The students are stunned by this bit of terribly bad news, and look around at one another and murmur their unhappiness and surprise. *Did I pick the wrong school?* they wonder.

'The problem,' the dean continues, 'is that as of today we don't know which half is right and which half is wrong. Because that's just how science works.'

Growth of Knowledge

We all face the same problem even if we're not studying to be doctors. A great deal of what we know to be true isn't true at all, and more will become obsolete or incorrect every day. This is one of the vexing problems of accelerating change, and it's highly disconcerting to have this happening to us continually. We ask in despair, *Is nothing stable?*

Alas, the answer these days is, *Maybe not so much.* This is the impact of the ever-expanding realm of knowledge on our mindset and on our decision making. And hence the awareness that we should avoid fixating on any particular thing we learned as of this morning, because it may not be so by this afternoon.

We must instead rigorously pursue knowledge, and be willing to set aside old knowledge and paradigms when new and more accurate ones emerge. This occurs with great regularity now, for the patterns that are emerging all speak to massive impacts from massive changes within the tumultuous process of the large scale economic shift.

44

EMERGENCE SHIFT
From the Random Comes the Unexpected

NEW PATTERNS

The final pattern that I'll discuss here in Part 2 is the phenomenon of emergence, a beautiful concept that has many important insights to offer us during this time of transition from one economy to the next.

The central insight of emergence is that complex systems consist of many individual actors, and as the actors have choice, the results of their interactions are not predictable. Instead, whatever happens emerges because they are connected and because they are interacting.

While this may seem to be a simple and obvious thing to say, its ramifications are highly significant because it describes the behavior of the important systems that constitute much of our society.

What systems are these? The economy is one, society itself is another, and natural ecosystems a third, all of which are vital to us and to our future. Systems like these are also referred to as 'complex, adaptive systems,' and the process of adaptation is precisely the process by which new characteristics and behaviors come about, or emerge, as their elements interact.

Interestingly, the more connections there are, the more possibilities there are for unexpected new states and behaviors to arise. Since those characteristics and behaviors haven't been seen before they're also 'unpredictable,' in the sense that they literally *cannot be predicted*. Surprises are thus the constant accompaniment in a time such as ours, surprises in both welcome and unwelcome variations.

As noted above in Section 39, the phenomenon of positive feedback drives a process of acceleration that speeds up the arrival of these surprises, sometimes so much so that we become numb. Or conversely, we seek to numb the pain through drugs and alcohol, the abuse of both of which is currently in the epidemic stage, and which should hardly be unexpected given the massive stress that we're all living under. But the things that emerge can also be good ones. Stress and change can motivate compassion and innovation, and can lead to new and unexpected solutions and opportunities.

The story of evolution is literally the story of emergence, for what is a mutation but an unforeseen, unplanned change that enables a new capability or a new behavior? Evolution has provided humans with big brains, and our big brains can plan and think and imagine in ways that our pre-human ancestors could not, from which one result is civilization, which is itself an expression of humanity's constantly adapting and changing responses to new situations and conditions.

The point of all this is that in our current period of accelerating change, in a time when so many major factors are interconnected as never before, and also obviously shifting in such a major way, the conditions are ripe for emergence, both good and bad. After all, a mutation can be beneficial but it can also make the organism less fit and more vulnerable. It's a roll of the dice that introduces possibly useful change into the narrow space that lies between the rigidity of total control and the scattered purposeless of utter chaos, that unique emergence zone where the most interesting things are found, including life, self-consciousness, civilization, and the economy.

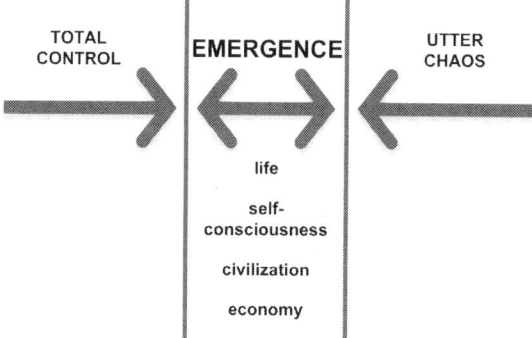

This means that all attempts to predict future outcomes or states in these systems are highly risky, and that consequently all decisions made in expectation of specific future conditions are also highly risky. In our current environment of accelerating change, this places very specific requirements on leaders, as they must shift their approach to planning and strategy from 'predicting the future' to 'preparing for possible futures,' a radically different skill that we will examine at length in Part 3.

▶

45

MINDSHIFT MAKERS

Our attitudes are shaped largely by our personal circumstances and histories, as well as by social, cultural, and economic experiences. If we are indeed shifting into a new society that operates within a new and digitized economic structure, and a massively robotized one, then we must anticipate fundamental shifts in experiences of attitudes about ... nearly everything. That is, we'll have to completely reconsider how the world works and what we may expect from it.

Of course the specifics will vary enormously depending upon where and how we live, and upon what we aspire to attain. Some seek personal fulfillment and enrichment, others seek monetary wealth, but billions just want not much more than survival from day to day and freedom from constant fear.

Many living in the developed nations during the first few generations following World War II experienced steadily increasing material abundance, while their children gained access to more education and opportunity than had ever been possible. Houses grew larger with each passing decade, ballooning in the U.S. from compact tract homes to mini-mansions three or four times larger. A garage for one car was became a garage for two and then three. Today it's common for none of the three to hold a car, because they're stuffed with an accumulation of even more junk that doesn't fit in the house, an overflow of massive material overabundance. When the garages are all full we rent storage lockers and pile still more stuff in there.

This is the result of rampant commoditization, enabled from the 1990s by the explosion of Asian manufacturing that pushes prices downward, hence the Wal-Mart slogan, 'Always Lower Prices.'

Material overabundance carries a high environmental cost, however, as materialist lifestyles serving millions and then billions of consumers require commensurate expansion in the logging of forests and the mining of ores, the burning of oil and coal to power the factories, cars, TVs, and computers, to light up the night and cool the hot days.

As we now understand, however, the rate at which industrial society consumes natural resources and turns them into waste is not sustainable, and thus we anticipate a shift of mindset from 'unlimited consumption' to a focus on quality rather than quantity, a shift from 'more' to 'better.' As attractive this may be in concept, it presents a difficult challenge for the mass production economy that relies on the consumption of ever more quantities to sustain its endless pursuit of GDP-measured growth.

But the basic structure of the economy is already shifting, an economics of digitalization is now being invented just as industrialism was invented from within the day to day pursuit of agriculture, and financialization grew from within industry.

As all this occurs, change will continue to accelerate, and our mindset must reflect this. As illustrated to the right, the actual rate of change is shown as the ascending exponential curve that accurately describes reality. But those who fail to grasp this perceive or expect a rate that's much slower. They are likely to fall into the linear mindset trap that will doom their enterprises by following 'the going out of business curve' (as aptly suggested by consultants Herman Gyr and Lisa Friedman). They will be left hopelessly behind.

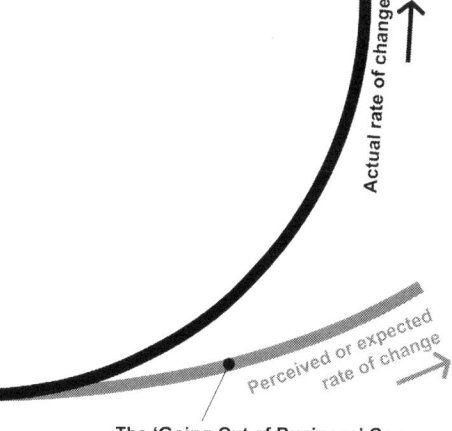

The 'Going Out of Business' Curve

Conversely, those who grasp that acceleration of change and digitalization are today's driving forces are thus already engaged in developing the newly required skills, as we will explore next in Part 3.

PART 3

SKILL SHIFT

Succeeding in the Digital Economy

As we understand that the world is shifting rapidly, and so we must develop a new mindset to bring our thinking and expectations into alignment with the new realities, and we must also consider how to best manage our enterprises, our families, our educations, and our careers, when the entire world is in the midst of this massive, shifting earthquake. There is nothing to do but learn the necessary skills, and then apply them, and contribute to the new economy/society/civilization that is emerging, the digital one.

The skills I focus on here aren't those related to professional practice in any particular field, in science or law, technology or engineering. They're not about how you practice medicine or accounting or government.

Instead, they're the essential skills that enable success in *all* these fields and in any field, necessary qualities and characteristics, focusing particularly on the development of strategy, leadership, organization, and innovation in the new digital economy.

SKILL SHIFT

STRATEGY

46

STRATEGY SHIFT
From Prediction to Possibility

When we think about what the future may bring as I did in Part 1, we realize that some of our expectations for what will happen will come true, but we also know that many will not. Some events and impacts will be less dramatic than we expect, or perhaps they won't occur at all. It's also plausible that some changes will arrive with an even greater crashing bang than expected, suddenly and in a more massive way, decisively and perhaps overwhelmingly.

Given that all these outcomes are entirely possible, what's the right perspective for a leader or strategist to adopt? How should we think about the future, and prepare for it? How do we create effective strategy?

Certainly the proper mindset is *not* to expect things to remain the same. We already discussed how futile this is, the ostrich's preferred way of coping, guaranteed to fail.

Conversely, we know that the future holds uncertainty, but how much? One way to visualize this is to consider what we call the 'cone of uncertainty,' a model of possible futures. Shown to the left are two versions, a narrow cone that suggests we expect the future to be pretty much like the present, or a wide open one indicating a wide range of possible futures. Of course it's the wide open one that gives the more accurate view.

The wide open cone suggests how difficult it is to make accurate predictions, as the range of possibilities is so gapingly vast that most predictions are bound to be wrong.

However, some leaders find it difficult to make this shift, because their (usually unspoken) expectation is that strategy must be based on predictions,

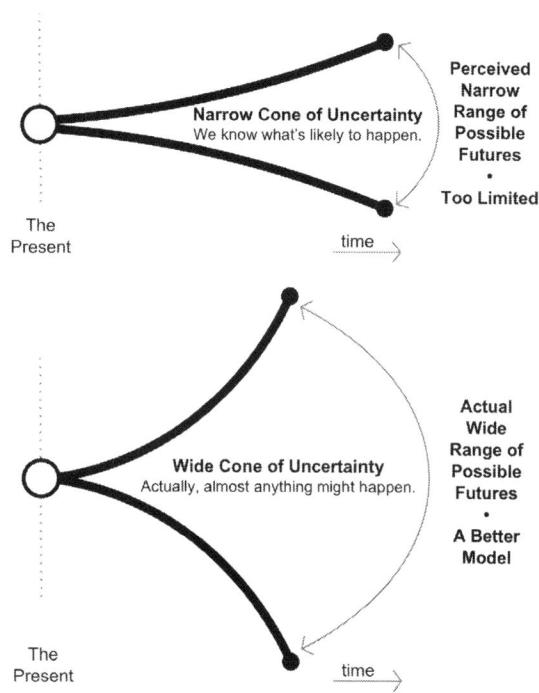

Two Cones of Uncertainty

even though as the more realistic cone of uncertainty shows, predictions made during times of rapid change are fraught with danger because they're so often incorrect, and developing strategies that rely on shaky predictions is even worse.

To succeed we must therefore shift our mindset away from 'making predictions' to 'examining future possibilities,' which constitutes excellent preparation for whatever does end up happening. This will alter how we think about the risks, problems, and opportunities that change presents, and how we respond when new and unexpected information arrives. Rather than fighting for the lost cause paradigm we can shift our focus to accepting change and embracing the new opportunities.

For example, although it's evident that robots are coming in a massive way, we don't know how badly they'll disrupt the economy, or how much they will enhance it. Will they free humans from tedious labor, or enslave us to debilitating unemployment and destitution? Possibility thinkers consider the full range:

- Will the world shift this way or that, or in yet another unenvisioned direction? What might result in each scenario?
- What are the possible directions in which the market could shift? What's the right business model in each case?
- What are the possible impacts of new technologies going to be? How can we get an early view of the emerging structures and patterns?
- How might attitudes and expectations change?
- Where could new competitors come from?

These are the right types of questions, open-ended ones that acknowledge multiple possibilities. It's then the strategist's job to develop worthwhile answers that model the possibilities rather than choosing preferences.

To enhance your capacity to cope with complexity (described next), skills including systems modeling and systems design (described following complexity) are essential to add to your own repertoire.

'Predictions of the future are never anything but projections of present automatic processes and procedures, that is, occurrences that are likely to come to pass if men do not act and if nothing unexpected happens.'

Hannah Arendt

47

COMPLEXITY SHIFT
From Connected to Omniconnected

STRATEGY

The story of the Big Shift is made immensely more complicated by the fact that every topic discussed in this book is in some way connected with every other one. Technology is related to urbanization is related to population is related to economy is related to climate is related to energy is related to work is related to attitudes is related to creativity and innovation ... and on and on it goes, endlessly looping.

And given that we're now all connected together into one stream of news and gossip and commerce and Twitter and Instagram, we see that all of human civilization operates in one gigantic feedback loop, and courtesy of the instantaneous nature of social media and global news, it connects in real time. This is omni-connectedness, all connected to all, the increasing interconnections that result in more interaction and more possibilities.

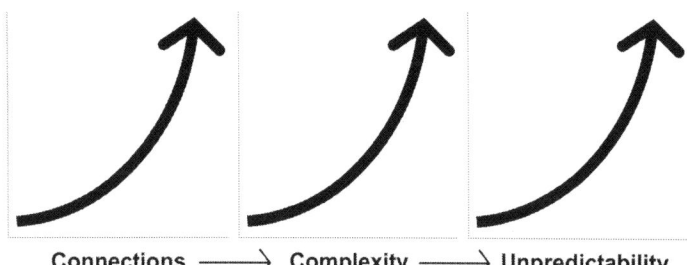

Connections ⟶ Complexity ⟶ Unpredictability

The more richly interconnected any system is, the more complex its range of possible behaviors, and since everything is connected to everything else *right now*, the range of possible behaviors is unlimited, a very thick soup of immense complexity. Change in one place often leads quickly to changes in others as the ricochets bounce through the system one after another, making also for increased unpredictability. (See the sidebar on the facing page.)

Complex interconnections define the global economy, given especially that the word 'economy' really just means 'the aggregate of everything related to production and consumption, trade, and wealth.' We know that the whole thing is incomprehensibly complex precisely because it is so deeply interconnected.

As we shift to the digital economy we inevitably see complexity continue to increase, which presents significant problems for managers who must design and decide, in addition to which complexity itself imposes a cost. As systems become increasingly complex the cost to operate them also increases, and at some point when the cost grows out of proportion to the benefits then it becomes an unacceptable burden.

This is a significant danger that digitalization and omni-connectedness may impose. But digitalization also offers potential solutions, some in the form of increasing efficiencies due to the ease of information flows, and in the shift of workstyles from centralized hierarchies to self-organizing networks, as we will consider below in Sections 53 - 58. If blockchains can remove 'friction' from the economy as it has been suggested that they can, then this will partially offset rising costs. And of course the speed of digital itself, instantaneous, also eliminates transaction costs (but increases the burdens on management to keep up, and forces a shift of leadership style, described next in Sections 48 - 52).

In the physical world, we see increasing complexity in cities, and as they continue to expand in population – millions of people, families, businesses, cars, trucks, buildings, animals, plants, and soon robots, all inhabiting a shared space – we will be challenged to reconcile conflicting goals and objectives that must be balanced through the intermediaries of social norms and governance.

'Complexity' is thus an important concept for us to grasp, because whenever we want to achieve anything we have to navigate skillfully through civilization's highly complex morass, or we just won't succeed.

Because complexity has increased so much during the recent decades due to economic globalization and to the vast increase in social connectivity, the capacity to cope with complexity itself has shifted from a desirable skill to an essential one. That capacity is often thought of as the ability to think in terms of and to manage both systems and ecosystems, as we will see next.

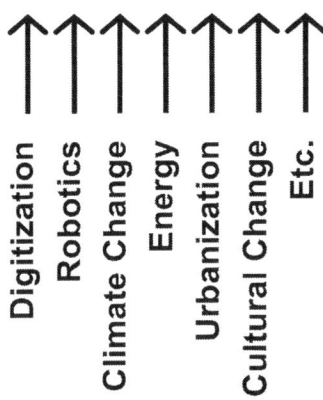

Increasing Complexity
All Shift, No Stasis

'In 2010 after a drought destroyed about one-fifth of Russia's wheat harvest, the Russian government banned wheat exports. That move, along with production declines in Argentina and Australia, which were also affected by drought, caused global grain prices to spike.

... In Egypt, annual food price inflation hit 19 percent in early 2011, fueling the protests that toppled President Hosni Mubarak.'

Joshua Busby
Foreign Affairs
July/August 2018

48

SYSTEM SHIFT
From Part Thinking to Ecosystem Modeling

STRATEGY

The full ensemble of business partners and competitors in the complex market setting constitutes an 'ecosystem,' a collection of entities that are mutually interdependent. They are separate but dependent upon one another. Similarly, the inhabitants and business in a city, or the plants and animals and insects in a rain forest also constitute complex ecosystems.

As I noted above, in the ever-expanding global economy we see the increasing interconnection of everything with everything else, and the more interconnected things become the more interdependent they become, and soon action in any one place affects many others, and soon everyone. As John Donne observed, none is alone and each effects all.

In organizations where everyone relies on the work outputs, creative contributions, and inspirations of others, it's apparent that no one succeeds by focusing only on their individual part of the system. Quite to the contrary, each one's success depends upon the success of the whole, and the whole is so massively interconnected inside and outside, which means that each individual must not only have awareness and understanding of the whole, but also the capacity to *act* effectively throughout the organization and across boundaries between all partner organizations. The challenge is that to assure our own success we thus have to manage the entire ecosystem, which is not a simple task.

A new field, 'systems thinking,' has emerged in recent decades to address exactly this problem. It teaches us the importance of a holistic perspective and provides skills needed to craft robust and useful models that enable us to better grasp complexity, and to understand that systems consist of interconnected parts that working together achieve systemic outcomes.

Systems models are all around us, and they play a role in every aspect of our lives. Do you use a map to get to your destination? That's a model of a system.

Do you use an organization chart, or a spreadsheet, or even a shopping list? Those are all models too. Much more complex models run on supercomputers to help us understand huge macrosystems such as the climate and the economy, aiding weather forecasters in anticipating hurricanes for example, and helping economists to make policy recommendations.

Systems thinking teaches us that to grasp the essence of any complex system – climate, economy, or market – it's never sufficient to look only at the parts. In fact it can be exceptionally counterproductive to look only at parts, because it is the connections between the parts and their integration as a whole that results in performance outcomes, good or bad. It's not because your car has 30,000 parts that it runs, but because those parts are properly connected into a whole system. Laying on the floor of the garage in a random pile, 30,000 parts can accomplish nothing.

Hence, system modelers must study and model the parts, their connections, *and* their wholes to understand complex systems, and thus to manage them effectively.

For example, an exceptionally productive systems model is the basis of Google's huge success. With an initial goal to simply improve web searching, the founders reasoned that the best way to optimize any search was to build a model of the entire world wide web. As a graduate student project, Google co-founders Page and Brin illicitly took over the Stanford University computer network to test their massive and still growing model, and it promptly crashed the network. Once they got their own hardware to test on, their model proved to be exceptionally useful, and as a result they are now two of the world's richest entrepreneurs. Their tool, Google, is basically a model of the entire internet ecosystem, 1.88 billion web sites (and growing each day), and it's the foundation of their subsequent megasuccess.

In its many forms, complexity is indeed the adversary of sound management, and systems thinking, modeling, and design are by far the best methods yet devised to address it. These are essential skills for success in the digital economy.

'The problems with which the universe can confront any society are, for practical purposes, infinite in number and endless in variety. As stresses necessarily arise, new organizational and economic solutions must be developed, typically at increasing cost and declining marginal return.

The marginal return on investment in complexity accordingly deteriorates, at first gradually, then with accelerated force. At this point, a complex society reaches the phase where it becomes increasingly vulnerable to collapse.'

Joseph Tainter
*The Collapse of
Complex Societies*

49

SYSTEM DESIGN SHIFT
From Assumptions to Models

STRATEGY

Significant suffering results when major social and environmental systems fail. Massive droughts cause the collapse of civilizations, provoke wars, and lead to mass starvation, while economic collapses cause widespread suffering as people lose homes, livelihoods, families, and often their sense of hope.

As we negotiate a world of complex social and economic landscapes in the midst of many challenges and in pursuit of our goals, the capacity to design effective systems has become an essential skill, and central to all systems designing is the development of simulations or models described above, which we make for the purpose of understanding them. The results of modeling efforts usually aren't perfect predictions, but they're much better than basing our decisions on untested assumptions or wishful thinking. As modeling skills and the computers they run on both improve, these forecasts get better and better, and help decision makers from national leaders to business leaders and families make better choices.

As I mentioned above, models are everywhere. Investors use market models to choose stocks, companies use demand forecasts to help determine which products to make based on what they expect customers to buy, hotels and airlines use models to predict occupancy rates and help set prices.

In fact, the act of management itself requires models. Management is the process of making decisions about what to do and what not to do, and *all decisions are essentially predictions* about the outcomes of future behaviors. All such predictions, and thus all decisions, are made based on models. The rub is often that the models are unconscious mental models, filled with untested biases or assumptions which events prove invalid. (See Section 42.)

This reminds us that the effectiveness and thus the utility of any model is unfortunately only fully evident after the fact, that is, when actual results are compared with forecast. Over time through care and attention, model and reality can become closely calibrated, enabling decision makers to have more trust in their models, enabling them to improve the designs of the systems modeled, and providing the basis for better decisions.

In preparing to make a decision, the process of developing the underlying model often proves invaluable because thinking through the parts and especially their connections and then representing them accurately in a model making tool is a tremendously important learning process.

An early and articulate practitioner of modeling was Jay Forrester, who created computer-based models of complex social systems like 'the economy' and 'the city' that helped shape strategies and policies for much better management.

One of his key insights was that complex systems often behave in ways we don't expect because their rich interconnections enable such a wide range of possible behaviors. This explains why so many intended solutions turn out badly, which he labeled as the tendency for 'counter-intuitive behaviors' to result from simplistic policy initiatives. His books and papers explain what good models are, how to create them, and how to then use them to design effective systems that avoid the counter-intuitive failures which overabundant complexity so often produces.

Forrester's tools and the concepts they inspired have proven invaluable not only for systems managers, but also in helping leaders to grasp essential qualities and characteristics that they must bring to their organizations.

'Many animals, from squirrels to rats to people, construct 'cognitive maps' of their spatial world, internal pictures of where things are in space, much like the external pictures of printed maps.

Once you represent spatial information in a map you can use that information much more flexibly and productively. A map lets you compare routes and discover the most efficient route, without actually having to take each one.'

Alison Gopnik
The Philosophical Baby

LEADERSHIP ▶ **50**

LEADERSHIP SHIFT
From Stability to Exploration

Everyone's life unfolds within a specific set of conditions, and as we acclimate to them they come to feel 'normal.' Frequently, however, we then mistakenly assume that the way it is now is the way it's always been and always will be. We are roused from this static and erroneous slumber when a shift occurs and we are forced by circumstances to confront assumptions that we formerly took for invariable realities. The world has changed.

Which is of course precisely what's occurring today.

As a new era dawns we have begun to experience the trends that are creating change and creating the characteristics of the new and different world. Although we don't yet know what tomorrow's full picture is going to be, leaders and strategists must pro-actively adopt new ways of thinking and working to avoid being overwhelmed by change. That is, they require a different mindset in order to be successful.

This notion is largely opposite from the traditional focus of organizational management, particularly in large firms and fattened bureaucracies. There, the goal is usually to achieve and then protect scale, scope, and continuity. From massive size, ever broader reach, and operational stability come profits, preferably huge ones, so firms seek to prolong the life of existing products and services and to maintain the uninterrupted stability of existing cash flows. To achieve this they seek to identify what will remain the same and they work hard to protect it.

In times of change, however, this is counterproductive. Indeed, in these times the most dangerous thing to do is to try to keep everything the same. Rather than resisting it, the success strategy is to constantly be alert for change, adapt to it, and even better is to create it.

Consequently, creativity and innovation are not just desirable skills, but essential ones, and the one energy that is primarily responsible for promoting, supporting, and enabling it is leadership, because it is leaders who communicate the necessity of being proactive rather than reactive, and who set in place processes and policies that enable organizations to search for and embrace the new, to explore, and to risk. Leaders thus set the tone and also initiate the necessary actions that enable the adaption and evolution of their enterprises.

Thus, instead of looking to assure that things remain the same indefinitely, which we know they will not, leaders must instead look to understand precisely what is changing, what will be different, and why.

The necessity of this way of working is not limited to leaders only. The embrace of change must reach deeply into the organization, for while leaders know a lot, others know a lot too, and the signals that portend change are usually noticed first at the front lines. Hence, a necessary and intentional shift must be made from adhering to the norms of the bureaucracy and the pursuit of stability in the hierarchy, to exploring, recognizing and responding to change.

Leaders who expect to sit contentedly atop the unchanging pyramid will not thrive in this new mode and mindset, and their organizations will suffer and decline. Conversely, those who actively seek out the new, the different, and the surprising will be prepared to seize new opportunities and abandon lost causes.

Hence, it wasn't an accident that one of Apple's most successful ad campaigns ever was built around the theme of 'Think Different,' and the company not only demonstrated how to think different, it 'did' different, and largely as a result it is today the most valuable corporation in the world.

Leadership plays an essential role in both thinking and doing differently, as no organization can innovate in spite of its leadership. Instead, innovation comes about *because* of robust leadership, and its commitment to exercising and perfecting the skills of creativity, exploration, and development.

51

ROLE SHIFT
From Controlling to Coaching

LEADERSHIP

A difficult challenge that leaders face in times of accelerating change and tumult is that their instinct is to try to bring more things into their control, to become involved in all decisions and thereby keep things moving in the right direction, but very often this is highly counter-productive. Paradoxically, the result of tightening control is that response times slow across the organization because people wait for leaders to decide, and while they're waiting things only get worse.

What usually works much better is to shift from 'controlling' to 'coaching.' When we think of organizations that compete in rapidly changing market environments as a lot like teams on the field of play, we understand that coaches can't control the actions of the players, but they do set the overall strategy of play, and through their leadership of practice they impart to the players an understanding of what's needed and expected in every facet of the game. And then the players must go onto the field and execute to the best of their abilities, competing against an opponent who's possibly done the same preparation, and so the flow of the game then reveals its results.

The importance of 'practice' is fully embedded in our concept of sports, where it plays the triple role of athletic conditioning, skill development, and enabling strategic execution. It's a given that youth teams practice, scholar-athletes practice, Olympians practice, and professionals practice, and it's not uncommon that over the course of a week the time spent in practice is ten or even twenty times longer than the duration of the game.

Unfortunately, practice is what's often omitted entirely from the preparation and strategic agenda setting of business leaders. Instead, business is often just execute-execute-execute, all game all the time. The predictable result is that skills erode, exhaustion sets in, and execution becomes repetitive. We repeat the old plays endlessly even though they're quite unsuited to the new situations. Of course during times of high stress and rapid change this is exactly the opposite of a success strategy.

Conversely, as with the best coaches in sports, leaders in business and life ensure that practice time is matched appropriately to game time. This preparation includes refinement of the strategic thinking that lies behind the design of the game plan, the strategy, as well as the adaptive adjustments that occur during the course of each game in response to what the opponent is doing, execution. After all, as the opponent's goal is the same as ours, we must match their adjustments and innovations with our own, or cede the advantage to them.

In this context the strategic importance of innovation becomes crystal clear. While strategy defines the goals and intentions, innovation becomes the essential means of execution, the way that we actually create the new products and services, processes and methods, insights and approaches that result in competitive advantage.

Interestingly, while the innovation process can and should be managed, the actual work of creating innovations cannot be controlled, in the sense that we cannot mandate that great ideas, insights, or new discoveries can occur at such-and-such a time. Instead, they must *emerge* through a rigorous process that balances the arts of curiosity, exploration, and discovery with the sciences of research, process management, and portfolio design. There is little here that can be controlled, and all attempts to do so kill the spirit of innovation that they're intended to promote.

There is, however, a very important role for guidance and coaching, and thus while the instinct to control may still be there, the much more effective role for leaders is to shift to coaching.

'The winner of the men's 200 meter race in the 1908 Olympics ran it in 22.6 seconds; today's high school record is faster by more than 2 seconds.

Today's best high school time in the marathon beats the 1908 Olympic gold medalist by more than 20 minutes. In diving, the double somersault was almost prohibited as recently as the 1924 Olympics because it was considered too dangerous. Today it's boring.

Contemporary athletes are superior not because they're somehow different but because they train themselves more effectively.'

Geoff Colvin
Talent is Overrated

52

SURPRISE SHIFT
From Knowing to Learning

LEADERSHIP

In a world of accelerating change, the value of any particular piece of knowledge is constantly shifting, as it may increase but it may also decrease. It may prove to be very important, or it could be entirely false and thus not knowledge at all.

This is nicely expressed in a story about the first day of medical school that I mentioned previously (Section 43). As you remember, the dean points out that half of what the students are about to learn is wrong, but unfortunately no one knows at present which half is which, so they're required to learn it all and then expected to later discard wherever is found to be erroneous.

This dilemma occurs as a consequence of the very nature of science, as new learnings and discoveries deepen our understanding and lead to improvements in the core knowledge as well as the guiding principles and models. Consequently, physicians are now required to engage in formal 'maintenance of certification' activities whereby they continually update their practical knowledge and demonstrate their up-to-dateness.

Leaders face the same challenge, the likelihood that what they think they know is no longer so. It's made worse by the fact that they became leaders by demonstrably applying their knowledge to meet successive challenges through the course of their careers, and now at the pinnacle it is often very difficult to recognize that the great accumulation of expertise that brought them to such levels of success may no longer even be relevant. Their organizations rely on them for their knowledge, and yet that very knowledge may have already become obsolete, or worse, erroneous and therefore counter-productive.

The success strategy is for leaders to therefore remain learners, or risk adding a final failure to the end of their resumes.

The shift from knower to learner is of course both a mindset and a skill, the mindset is the acceptance of the condition, and the skill is active engagement in learning.

One tool that serves them well is the practice of 'reverse mentoring.' Mentoring is the process by which the more experienced guide the less experienced; reverse mentoring is based on the awareness that the young may be less experienced and knowledgeable overall, but the experiences and knowledge they do have are highly relevant to the challenges of the present and future. Through sharing of technical expertise and social experiences with one another, both benefit.

Another dimension of this dilemma is how we handle it when we discover that what we thought to be true is no longer the case. Jonathan Ive, Apple's Chief Design Officer and a key leader during the last twenty years of Apple's ascent to the pinnacle of world commerce has expressed this in a compelling and insightful way. In commenting about the work of his design team he noted that, 'One of the hallmarks of the team is inquisitiveness, being excited about being wrong because that means you've learned something new.'

Ive's remark shows both the mindset and the skill, attitude and practice, and it has contributed significantly to Apple's capacity to conceive of and bring to market entirely new technology that is startlingly original. 'Learning something new' enables a foundation of exceptional creativity, and the quest for it and the capacity to transform learnings into value is the essence of creativity in the new economy.

It's rare to hear a senior executive expressing enthusiasm about being wrong, but it's obviously one of the characteristics that distinguishes Apple, and it also distinguishes great leaders as great learners from the rest. Having adopted this attitude, the leader's next task is to develop organizations capable of fulfilling their visionary potential.

ORGANIZATION ▶ **53**

ORGANIZATION SHIFT
From Making Stuff to Making Meaning

Most of the giant industrial firms of the 20th century were organized according to a clear and very explicit separation of hierarchically-defined rules and roles. The large mass of workers were there 'to do their job,' and thinking was definitely not included in the job description; that was the responsibility of someone else. It seems strange to read this today, yet if you go back and read the histories you find that a very distinct line was drawn between 'working,' which 'workers' did, and 'thinking,' which bosses did.

Today's situation is exactly the reverse. Now thoughtfulness is valued over nearly every other quality because not only is universal thoughtfulness desirable, in fact it's entirely necessary in order to cope successfully with increasing complexity and the acceleration of change.

The value of thoughtfulness may be best exemplified by Toyota, which for decades has nurtured an organizational culture in which each individual's thoughtful contributions were not only welcomed, they were expected. Of course Toyota's main business is making cars, and cars are built on massive assembly lines consisting of thousands of workers who perform tasks that are repetitive. How easy it would be to become lost in mindless repetition.

While workers in Ford and GM assembly plants openly commented that, 'You get my body, but you're not paying for my brain,' a Toyota worker has the opposite expectation. One of the best management books ever written, *40 Years; 20 Million Ideas,* describes the Toyota Suggestion System, which year after year made the company better, more efficient, more productive, and more satisfying to work in. It's exactly this mindset that enabled Toyota to develop and perfect the most advanced manufacturing system the world has ever seen, now imitated everywhere, but originated in Japan through a commitment to universal thoughtfulness. The days of just 'doing a job' are done; now what matters is how you add value, and how much.

Looking ahead, we're not sure if robots will do only mindless and repetitive work or if they will do it in an observant and thoughtful manner, noticing deficiencies and fixing them as they go. But we can be 100% sure that the essential role for people will be in creating value by applying humanity's unique qualities and capabilities to observe, empathize, problem-solve, and optimize, to do so with sensitivity, care, compassion, and creativity, across multiple dimensions including socially, culturally, and humanely. That is, we will strive for personal satisfaction, accomplishment, and development, as well as the advancement of society and civilization, which is the process of creating meaning.

Thus, the organizational effort shifts from 'doing a job' to 'adding value,' from making yet more stuff, to making richer meanings.

54

WORK SHIFT
From Solo to High Performance Team

ORGANIZATION

While creative expression in the arts is often a solo effort, most creative work in other fields has shifted definitively to teams. This has occurred largely because the increasing complexity of most of today's problems, situations, products, services, machines, and technologies exceed the scope and competence of any one person. Consequently, teamwork has become the normal and necessary way of getting work done for all types of organizations, from businesses to governments, and from small firms to large ones.

Health care, for example, is no longer organized around the heroic MD, the medical professional working alone. Instead we see 'interprofessional' health care collaboration, through which the knowledge, insights, and capabilities of nurses, doctors, pharmacists, medical assistants, therapists, administrators, and social workers are all aligned to enable the success of each patient's treatment. Why the shift? Because providing health care in an interprofessional team achieves better health outcomes, at lower cost, with less stress, and with more professional satisfaction.

Software programming is a team process, too, using Agile methodology and its embedded concepts of the 'scrum team' that works together to achieve carefully defined targets, and work organized in stages known as 'sprints' wherein teams collaborate directly with end users to create useful code. (See the following Section.)

Innovation researchers work in teams because so many scientific, technical, and business disciplines have to be integrated in order to create new solutions, and because speed matters so much in the competitive market, and integrated teams make progress so much faster than slow committees can possibly attain.

Hollywood's 'gig economy' organizes films as projects made by teams of independent professionals who work together for a few months and then disband and move on to other projects.

Indeed, more and more forms of intellectual work are taking on this quality, which foretells not only a new form of organization, but new types of offices. Co-working spaces that look like Starbucks serve the new economy of team-based work with open plan spaces that individuals, teams, and start-up companies use by the hour, the day, or the month.

Diverse teams are much more creative, more innovative, and often more productive than homogenous teams or individuals working alone. These teams are composed of people with different and complementary skills, from different backgrounds, with different worldviews.

To save time, complex work tasks are addressed not in a linear and sequential, step by step manner, but in an integrated flow and in parallel as much as possible. Since your outputs are my inputs, and my outputs are your inputs, we progress together, mutually dependent, and we achieve better outcomes, too.

While we might define 'cooperation' as the capacity to work together harmoniously, the shift from individuals to high performance teams that I'm describing here is something deeper. Call it 'integration' or 'deep collaboration' to invoke the notion that we are striving for something far beyond good or average. We intend to work together in a profound way, as the end point we aim for is brilliant work achieved through high performance.

'Creative activities in companies are not complete merely with the completion of the sequence of planning/developing, testing, and producing. They are only complete when the actual goods/services have been provided to customers who make effective use of them and place the anticipated value upon them.

Creative activities in companies may therefore be envisaged as spreading outward in succession from the individual level to the group level, corporate level and finally to the user level.

To achieve this expansion, an interpersonal empathy with the activities and their results must be induced at each stage of transition. The greater this empathy is, the wider the circle of the creative activities and the higher the value created for the company and for society.'

Teruyasu Murakami
and Takashi Nishiwaki
Strategy for Creation

55

AGILE SHIFT
From Slow to Nimbly Fast

Today's market dynamics reward the speedy, but oh how they do punish the slow. It will be the same tomorrow. Being first to market yields exceptional advantages as long as you're first with the right stuff, and thus in Silicon Valley it's widely understood that if you're not first or second to market, you might as well go home and find something else to do.

Effective strategy and foresight provide essential insights and guidance to all facets of the organization by defining what should be done, but then you actually have to do it, implement it, and do it fast, because your competitors may have arrived at exactly the same insights already.

The goal, then, is to be fast to create the right new products, services, and business models without a lot of wasted effort, to progress nimbly without spinning your wheels. Since the work that needs to be done quickly is becoming progressively more complex, accomplishing this is no simple feat.

In the previous section I mentioned that Agile techniques were pioneered for software development, and that offer very specific tools for gaining speed while enhancing quality. Invented by a team of experienced programmers who felt extremely frustrated with the tedious progress their field was achieving on large projects, and embarrassed over the frequent and highly publicized failures of multi-hundred-million-dollar software systems, they created the Agile methods that have proven quite useful for all types of work that require deep thinking, creative insight, and rapid innovation. The power of Agile is achieved through a few simple principles and practices that are easy to apply.

- *Teaming:* Agile is a team-based approach, which we already know is how much great work gets done. Agile provides very helpful guidance on team size, interactions, and project management. (More on this in the next section.)

- *Sprints:* Projects are organized as short segments called sprints that last a few weeks or less, with clearly defined goals and specific deliverables that help optimize the effort while eliminating wasted effort and time.

- *Prioritization:* The work undertaken in each sprint is that which has been identified as the strategically most important, which keeps projects focused on maximum value creation and keeps them from getting bogged down in minutiae and trivia.

- *Customer Engagement:* Customers (or users) work along side during all phases of design and implementation to assure that the work we're doing actually provides value.

- *Completion:* Every sprint consists of deliverables that are clearly defined at the outset, and progress against them is tracked on a daily basis on the immensely valuable 'burn-down chart,' which gives immediate visual feedback on progress vs. plan.

- *Transparency:* Like all creative workers, programmers are independent and intensely dislike doing administration. To simplify things they prepare a simple report at the end of each day that summarizes their progress against their specific targets, enabling managers and indeed the entire team to know immediately if any of the work is falling behind so resources can be shifted to address the gaps.

- *Meetings:* Do you like endless meetings? Most people hate them too. Agile uses a daily ten minute check-in that is done standing up to avoid the temptation to lean back, chatter, and waste time. Necessary design meetings are managed with great intention and kept to a minimum.

- *Retrospectives:* The retrospective (or 'innospective') is a rigorous meeting the purpose of which is to assess results and performance after every sprint, which assures that the learning process is embedded as a continual focus, and thus improvement in skills, teamwork, and project management is also continual.

Agile techniques aren't the only skills that increase speed, but they do make a tremendous difference across all activities that engage us in teamwork, hard thinking, and heavy duty innovation. Since speed matters so much in the new marketplace you can reasonably think of them as essential.

Here's what we avoid by applying Agile:

'The time spent on any item of the agenda will be in inverse proportion to the sum of money involved.'

C. Northcote Parkinson

'80% of the time of 80% of the people who participate in any given meeting is wasted.'

Bartleby's Law

'In 80% of meetings, the decisions taken will be in line with the highest-paid person's opinion.'

The HIPPO Law

56

POWER SHIFT
From Hierarchy to Network

ORGANIZATION

The hierarchical form of organization was invented millennia ago to protect and preserve established powers in government, military, and church. It remains the predominant organizational form today, the standard way of structuring and managing all types of organizations.

Skills and behaviors related to these power dynamics have been developed over centuries, and we might even say they've been perfected. Qualities that matter most in a hierarchy are power and authority, and people of course fight hard to preserve these prerogatives. Consequently, the primary orientation of the hierarchy is its vertical axis, the co-called 'chain of command.' Decisions and instructions flow 'downward' from leaders to workers; questions and requests flow 'upward.'

Since information travels 'up' and 'down' the chain of command to assure that leaders are fully informed and always 'in the loop' on all actions and decisions, the things that often get insufficient attention are the new ideas, the hazy glimpses of impending change, and the surprising insights. Alas, they're just not important enough to bother the hierarchy with.

But the challenge that massive and hierarchical organizations face in times of rapid change is that they continue to execute as though nothing had changed, operating in what becomes a mindless manner because their metrics and rewards are aligned around repetition and execution rather than difference and innovation. Thus, they keep doing the same wrong thing over and over when what they most need is to adapt and innovate, to rethink and change.

Consequently, while it serves some purposes well, the hierarchy's shortcomings are becoming more problematic because the two factors that hierarchies typically do not handle well, external change and internal innovation, are precisely the defining characteristics of our time. Thus, the same qualities that make hierarchies strong in stable times are the ones that

'The old organization was built around control, but the world has changed. The world is moving at such a pace that control is a limitation. It slows you down. You've got to balance freedom with some control, but you've got to have more freedom than you ever dreamed of.'

Jack Welsh
Former CEO of GE

'The command and control model of leadership just won't work 99 percent of the time.'

Alan .G. Lafley
Former CEO of
Procter & Gamble

make them fatally weak during periods of turbulence, like today.

To meet the new requirements of a changing world, it turns out that 'networks' perform far better than hierarchies because they have many particularly desirable qualities. For instance, networks are self-organizing, forming spontaneously as people locate the others they need to engage with to accomplish meaningful work. Trust, reputation, and ability are foundational elements of a network; you earn your way in by your competence and trustworthiness, or out by their lack.

Hierarchy
Top-Down

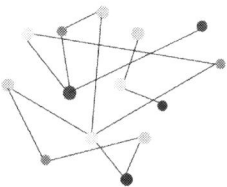

Network
Self-Organizing

Information also propagates differently in a network than in a hierarchy. It's shared as needed with no consideration as to 'up' or 'down,' and as a result the new information that any person in a network discovers is shared very rapidly with exactly the person who needs to know. This occurs because the network knows who needs to know – that's what makes it an effective network. This of course facilitates and expedites the development of solutions that hierarchies would never discover. Thus, recognizing when something has changed, sorting out the options, and delivering the right responses is what networks do exceptionally well.

In addition, when their purposes are fulfilled or evaporate, networks evaporate also, so they rarely become organizational overhead but instead operate as services to the hierarchy that are essentially free, a parallel world in which innovation and problem solving are the norm, and overhead is low.

As networks are a critically powerful means for recognizing and responding to change, they create value far out of proportion to their costs. Thus, it's only a small exaggeration to suggest that a hierarchy is a power-based organization that is designed for saying 'no,' while a network is a competence-based capacity that self-organizes for creating 'yes.'

Consequently, empowering and enabling networks to operate inside of hierarchies is an exceptionally sound organizing strategy.

'We now have communications tools that are flexible enough to match our social capabilities, and we are witnessing the rise of new ways of coordinating action that take advantage of that change.'

Clay Shirky
Here Comes Everybody

57

EXTREME SHIFT
From Team to Skunkworks

ORGANIZATION

In my recent book *Foresight (Foresight and Extreme Creativity: Strategy for the 21ˢᵗ Century)* I included the phrase 'extreme creativity' in the title because I wanted to make the point that the large and systemic problems we face will be successfully met not just by regular old every day creativity, which is fine, but by the extreme form that outperforms the normal to become supernormal. This was also intended to draw attention to the complex nature of the challenges we face, and to propose that going forward we will organize and concentrate creative efforts to address the very biggest problems we face, such as mitigating the effects of climate change, building the new global energy infrastructure for human civilization, counteracting urban sprawl, cleaning up pollution, and overcoming rampant poverty, rising inequality, social injustice, etc.

'Extreme creativity' is a way of working in teams formed specifically to address these tough problems, especially when we realize that it's foolish to wait around for someone else to get interested and take it on, when we ought to be doing that ourselves, now.

In the aerospace industry, teams like this are sometimes created in urgent situations and given an old hangar to work in somewhere off in the back corner of an airfield where no else bothers to go. Happily left alone, they work quickly by testing and experimenting, failing fast to succeed fast, and because their way of working is a bit unorthodox they quickly gain the highly honored name of 'skunkworks.'

Skunkworks teams often produce great ideas at a far higher rate than average or even above-average groups of engineers because their way of working is superior, and because team members experience great joy, high satisfaction, and total commitment. The very long hours they work don't seem so bad because the work is important, fellow team members are inspirational and fully engaged, and the sense of accomplishment is so profound.

Who's on these teams? Members of a skunkworks are the ones who can perform, who can get the job done, which means you don't end up on a team like this unless someone who's already on the team thinks you belong there too. Hence, it's a matter of 'what you know' *and* 'what you can do.'

As a result, these teams tend to be exceptionally diverse. Competence knows no color, no ethnicity, no gender, it cares only about skill and commitment and the capacity to get the job done.

People who excel at their work are naturally drawn to a skunkworks, while conversely people who don't work at a consistently high level naturally fall away.

Working in this way, projects that might otherwise take months, years, or decades under 'normal' (read 'mediocrity') circumstances can somehow get accomplished in a skunkworks in weeks, even when dealing with limited resources. Or sometimes, necessity being the mother of invention that it is, *because* of limited resources.

So why don't we organize all the work this way? Well, we can, and we ought to. We've got major challenges to address, and this is most likely the best way to do it.

When Boeing developed its new 777 aircraft in the early 1990s the project was organized as essentially a giant skunkworks. More than 5000 staff members were divided into teams, and each team had its own dedicated work space. This work style, high levels of coordination, and waves of innovation converged to produce one of the most successful projects the company had ever undertaken. It went so well that the project leader, Alan Mulally, became the next CEO of Ford, where he also achieved great success.

Boeing obviously missed him terribly, because its next big project, the 787, became mired in engineering and production problems and was finally delivered years late and billions over budget.

Karl Sabbagh
21st Century Jet

58

WORKSTYLE SHIFT
From My Work to Teamwork

ORGANIZATION

Since so much of the most important work is done in teams, the approach each individual takes to attain their own personal success naturally shifts from a focus on 'my work' to aligning, organizing, and optimizing 'teamwork.' We can't merely tolerate each other if we depend upon each other for our mutual success, and since our organization depends on the quality of our teamwork for its success.

The importance of great teamwork has led to some pretty interesting tactics to make sure it's built into the everyday way of working. In addition to promoting network-style thinking and enabling skunkworks, some very savvy start-up companies organize their works spaces in clusters composed of people who do different jobs and work in different departments. This very smart use of office space promotes teamwork, learning, collaboration, and high performance by ensuring that people progressively learn more about the work outside of their specific domain, thus promoting better cross-functional collaboration and a richer social environment also.

The shift from my work to teamwork also means that the focus of performance assessment shifts from individuals to teams. Through tools like the 360 degree assessment, inquiry in all directions involves teammates, peers, networks, and up and down the hierarchy in a more holistic view of the work and the workers. The intent of these assessments also shifts, away from criticism and fault finding and identifying 'why someone is not meeting expectations,' to coaching for performance improvement along with enhanced satisfaction.

In the Agile process described in Section 55, the comparable process is called the 'retrospective' (or 'innospective'), the dialog to examine the quality work that has just been completed and to reflect on the way the work was done, including factors such as communication, teamwork, decision making, and coordination, with the specific intent of learning and improving.

Military organizations conduct a similar process called 'after action review' after every engagement, because learning and improvement based on the rich experiences of an action just completed may equate to future survival.

The shared workspace cluster, the 360 degree review, the retrospective, and the after action review, each of these is an organizational technique that reflects the evolving nature of work and of value creation, the shift of focus from me to us, from *my work* and *my success* to *our work* and *our shared accomplishments.*

In the complex and highly interconnected fields, domains, and markets of the emerging economy, each individual's capacity to create value is leveraged and enhanced by their participation in high performance teams, which is often how the greatest things are accomplished.

INNOVATION ▶ **59**

INNOVATION SHIFT
From Luck to Rigor

A quick recap. Our exponentially-changing world is making the transition from an industrial economy to a much different digital one, a momentous shift that brings with it enormous complexity, great opportunities, and also great risks. We have explored many of the specific component shifts and considered how they aggregate into an overall one, and we have also recognized that all of this requires of us a new mindset, the capacity to cope with and manage change, as the days of stability are no more.

Here in Part 3 we've examined strategy, leadership, and the organization, and now we come to the critical action step, innovation. For it is through innovation, and innovation alone, that strategizing and planning and thinking come together into doing, into creating the new products and services and business models and systems that will enable sustained success. Without innovation you're probably doomed; with it you may well triumph.

In this section and the 11 that follow, then, I'll describe the essential elements of the innovation system that's proven effective at creating exceptional value in all kinds of organizations, and all around the world.

The acts of innovation create the shifts, and to succeed in the new economy we must become more effective shift makers, or in a word, to be effective innovators. The resulting innovations embody that marvelously elusive yet curiously evocative quality of newness that elicits excitement, intrigue, and sometimes inspiration. Innovation is the new and different when it is also better, when it expresses and provides something that did not previously exist. Such value can take many forms: innovation can yield a product or process, a policy, a technology, or a technique. It may also benefit society rather than creating profits for companies, but whether for profit or for social good, in the end to qualify as an innovation, to be worthy of that name, it has to add value for someone other than the creator: an end user must benefit. Innovation value is experienced and attributed by its buyers and users, not by its conceivers and makers.

It's true that some things we label as innovations are superficial and frivolous, fads and trinkets that don't at all deserve to be called innovative. But the ones that are vital to who we are and how we live constitute a long and unforgettable list that we rely upon every day: plows and seeds and cities, electricity and power plants and batteries, computers and telephones and iPhones, tractors and cars and airplanes, rockets and satellites and GPS, refrigerators and power tools, vaccines and medicines and fertilizers, water purifiers and antibiotics and anesthesia, and on and on the list goes.

Businesses that create innovations thrive, and nations that innovate often gain tremendous advantages, while those that fail to innovate may also fail outright, and disappear.

So how is innovation accomplished?

Innovation is a skill, and like every skill it can be studied and mastered. Innovation can also be managed, and indeed it *must* be managed since so much depends on it. For if it's not managed rigorously, then innovation occurs only as random luck, and who would think that random efforts are either sufficient or prudent?

The rigorous pursuit of innovation is guided by the knowledge that success requires us to balance the open-ended flow of creativity with prescriptive stages of disciplined inquiry. In its most robust form, innovation is a discipline that creates new possibilities for the future by structuring the inquiry into the unknown which in turn creates new knowledge and new possibilities. It is driven from within by intrinsic aspirations and commitments, and guided from without by rigorous questioning, effective methods, and strong leadership.

'People who rank high for intrinsic motivation on various psychological tests consistently produce work that is judged more creative in studies. Conversely, people who work in professions demanding creativity (artists, research scientists) reliably rank higher on tests of intrinsic motivation.'

Geoff Colvin
Talent is Overrated

60

INNOVATION PLANNING SHIFT

From Random to Systematic

INNOVATION

The Innovation Plan is the detailed operating model that describes how you manage the innovation process rigorously, and it also defines the contents of your innovation portfolio. I will say a bit about both.

The Innovation Process: As I've mentioned in previous sections and especially regarding Organization Shift (Sections 53 – 58), innovation is a demanding process that addresses a complex market environment. It's difficult for most organizations to do it well because the essential requirements for success at innovation include being open-ended, accepting uncertainty, promoting curiosity and creativity (which we will explore shortly), the willingness to take certain forms of risk, and being fast. None of these are strengths of the traditional hierarchy, which means that innovation in the corporation often happens only at random, which is of course not at all sufficient.

Five essential questions shape the systematic innovation process, beginning simply with *'Why?'* Why do we innovate? It is of course because we must do so to survive. (An added plus is that it's great fun!) Innovation is an essential element of our strategy, and it is informed by knowledge of emerging trends and carefully crafted scenarios that help us understand emerging patterns.

'What' we do is to design and manage our innovation portfolio by considering key factors such as the importance of business model innovation, and by preparing detailed technology roadmaps that guide us into the future. *'How'* is the process of generating great ideas and then transforming them into value, in which we apply techniques like design thinking to gain deep understanding of the context of our customers' lives and to come up with great solutions to meet their stated and hidden needs.

'Who' is the innovation culture in our organization and throughout our

ecosystem, the people who are enthusiastic participants in all this innovation effort, and *'where'* is the tools and techniques applied.

You noticed that I left off the sixth question, *'when,'* but you already know why that is – *'when'* is certainly *'now.'*

The figure to right shows these elements aligned in a useful process framework. It's also described in considerable detail in a series of four books, *Permanent Innovation, The Agile Innovation Master Plan, The Innovation Formula,* and *Agile Innovation.* Many organizations worldwide are using this framework to bring rigor and proficiency to their innovation efforts.

The Innovation Portfolio: The innovation portfolio is an essential tool for managing the balance between risk and reward. Too much risk, of course, could endanger the organization. But so could too little, because if we make only small steps then we will likely miss the big shifts, resulting in the major strategic risk of being left behind.

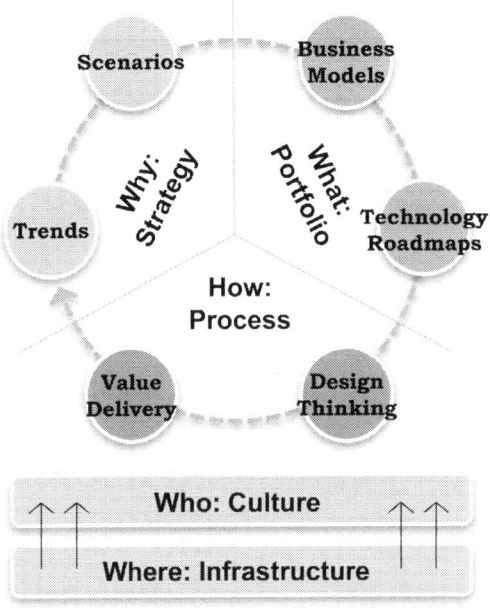

A Rigorous Innovation Planning Framework

A poignant example of this is Nokia, which in 2007 was the world's leading cell phone maker. A self-congratulatory memo from late 2007 showed the company's full line of cell phones, beautifully arrayed in a handsome setting. At about that time Apple introduced the first iPhone, which Nokia publicly and privately panned. The one characteristic that all the Nokia phones shared and which was notably absent from the iPhone was the keypad, which as you know was replaced by the iPhone's super useful touch screen. Nokia scoffed, believing that 'it's not a phone without a keypad.' Nokia's innovation portfolio apparently didn't take touch screens seriously, a painful example of insufficient risk taking, complacent business modeling, and inadequate technology roadmapping that, along with its condescending attitude, doomed the company.

In the following sections we'll look in detail at the essential elements shown in the diagram, *trends, scenarios, business models, technology roadmaps,* and *design thinking,* and learn how they enable the shift from random to systematic innovation, and thus to the creation and delivery of exceptional value.

61

TREND SHIFT
From Hindsight to Foresight

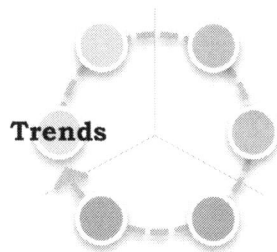

Trends

INNOVATION

As we embark upon the rigorous innovation effort we realize that we're making a shift from hindsight, looking backwards, to foresight, as we seek a clear grasp on the emerging trends and technologies, the strategies, policies, and then the innovations that are shaping the future of industry and the economy.

Applying the mindset of the learner enables us to recognize that whatever we know today is likely to be different tomorrow, and so we constantly seek insight into new trends, discoveries, breakthroughs, and competitors. We continually scan for new ideas in the systematic effort of information gathering, we develop extensive learning networks with partner firms and universities, and with firms that service and support new businesses, to learn what the entrepreneurs are doing. We go on research and trend safaris and even do some window shopping and mall walking, all to broaden our perspective on what is and isn't possible today, and to reveal what may become common tomorrow.

Over-the-horizon radar, also called 'weak signal research,' is a great starting point, looking beyond traditional limits to discover what may otherwise be hidden. Done well, this research yields a rich collection of impressions and insights, but they may not organize themselves into a coherent set of actionable patterns. For that we must create new maps of future territories, disruption maps.

Disruption maps identify where breakthroughs, disruptions, and new business models are likely to come from, approximately when, and in what clusters. The essential value here is not so much because we expect these predictions to be accurate (we know how unlikely that is), but because we're thinking about the trends and patterns of the unfolding future, and this will undoubtedly inform our planning and decision making.

We might ask,

- What events and technologies will lead to what new market opportunities?
- What shifts cause which threats and disruptions?
- Who are the future players and what are their goals likely to be?

These are all important questions to consider, and by mapping them you may also discover how important new forces and factors may arise. This will then cause you to rethink assumptions and expectations, always a hugely valuable exercise.

As time progresses and you compare your disruption maps with the actual flow of emerging trends you gain deep insights into the patterns of change, providing a much better foundation for your subsequent strategic planning and innovation execution.

For example, a disruptive trend that's already having considerable impact is the development of 3D printing, or the Maker Bot, a manufacturing device that can be as small as a microwave oven, and which can be used to create just about anything. How will this technology impact the market? Let's explore it in the next section, 3D Shift.

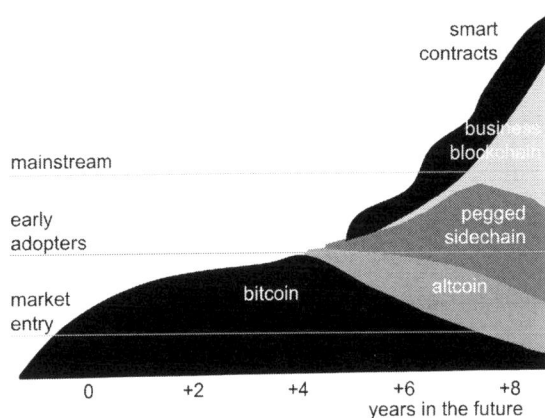

BitCoin / BlockChain Disruption Map
From Market Entry to Mainstream

62

3D SHIFT
From Consuming to Creating

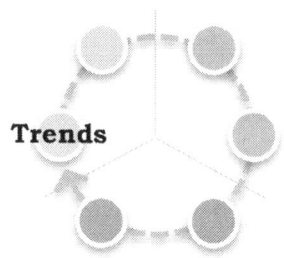

Trends

INNOVATION

Two major economic trends most clearly characterized the 20th century: the aggregation of ever more knowledge, and the centralization and globalization of nearly all economic activity. The pace of knowledge aggregation due to advances in science and technology shows no sign of slowing, and as noted above, more scientists are alive today and still working than in all of previous human history combined. What can they possibly do but create still more knowledge? And what will that knowledge do but result in ever more change?

As their numbers grow and the fruits of their work lead to the continuing refinement and specialization of science into narrower domains, sub-domains, and sub-sub-domains we gain more and more knowledge about more and more of the universe. Today there are already hundreds of specialized scientific journals, each charting progress in yet another field of discovery, and new ones are added each year as science continues to expand.

Simultaneously, the tools of science just keep getting better. Interestingly, while particle physics has gotten wildly more expensive with new colliders now costing billions of dollars, other fields have gotten progressively cheaper. As we saw above, the first full human genomic sequence cost $2.7 billion. In 2008 it cost $10 million, and today it can be done for about $1000 or less, and you'll have the results in a day.

The phenomenal improvement in computer chips enables this, ever faster and cheaper year by year. All devices that rely on computer chips for basic functionality have followed the same cost/improvement dynamic, which is why a 3D printer now costs $100 to $1000, and can do the work that used to require, well, a factory. Today you can print yourself a pair of custom shoes in about an hour, or use a bigger machine to print yourself a modest-sized house in about 20 hours. Yes, now you really can now 'print' a house.

This do-it-yourself trend is the 'maker movement,' which has implications not only for those who want to do it themselves, but for everyone. For example, it costs millions of dollars to send up just a tiny little part to repair a who-knows-what on the International Space Station, but now that there's a 3D printer on the ISS many repairs will cost a lot less. In the future, of course, NASA intends to print entire moon bases and Martian outposts, while back on the good old Earth you and your children may get so accustomed to making your own stuff that the entire process of shopping and buying could become fundamentally disrupted.

And it's already happening, although in another way. Do you have a Facebook page to express your unique self, or a YouTube channel or a blog or a LinkedIn page? All of these elements compose your digital identity, and by creating them you're developing and expressing your own brand, and thereby shifting from being a passive consumer to an active creator.

Combining the functionality of advanced robotics with self-driving vehicles and 3D printing will transform how products are designed, manufactured, *and* delivered, enabling unprecedented specialization and customization at ever larger scales, perfectly expressing creativity in the digital economy. At the San Francisco Public Library they're already using 3D printers to create new, custom prosthetic limbs for homeless amputees at a tiny fraction of what it used to cost, creating enormous social benefit for people without much means and who previously didn't have much hope.

It won't be long before 3D printers are as common as refrigerators and dishwashers, but cheaper, thus providing another technology that transforms shoppers into designers, buyers into makers, and consumers into creators.

This is but one example of the rich universe of ideas to uncover when you go trend hunting, the immensely valuable experience that richly seeds the innovation process.

And what shall we do with this information? An important next step is to create scenarios, models of the future that expose new threats and possibilities in the emerging patterns of change.

63

SCENARIO PLANNING SHIFT
From Predictions to Possibilities

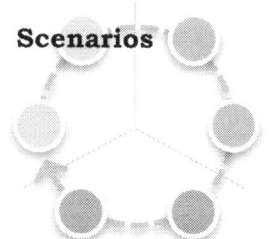

Scenarios

INNOVATION

Scenario planning is a rigorous thinking and planning tool that's used to transform data and information about trends into robust insights about the future. The goal is not to predict what will happen (which is fruitless), but rather to understand what could happen under a variety of different sets of conditions. Scenario planning is thus the skill partner to the 'possibility mindset' described in Section 46.

Scenario planning was invented to help leaders and managers move beyond the narrow and limiting modes of 'prediction thinking' and to enable the much more potent mode of *possibility thinking*. It's based on the realization that predictions are very rarely accurate, and that strategies based on inaccurate predictions are simply dangerous. After all, if the prediction is off then the strategy based upon it well likely prove to be counterproductive. A much better approach is anticipating and exploring many possibilities, as this trains the mind not to fixate on one expected future, but rather to be diligent about gathering facts (not assumptions) about what's really happening, and responding quickly as the picture comes into focus.

The technique of scenario planning was developed at Royal Dutch Shell during the 1960s, and has served the company well since then by educating the company's leadership about the unpredictable flow change, while also enhancing the important capabilities of flexibility and adaptation. It has also yielded powerful insights about shifts in Shell's core energy markets that have enabled the company to respond well to significant challenges.

Scenario planning is equally useful outside of the corporate context. A scenario planning activity conducted during the apartheid era in South Africa helped the country's leaders discover that a very narrow pathway lay between national disintegration and civil war, and proved invaluable in helping to sustain peace during the difficult transition to democracy.

Given the heightened uncertainties we face today, scenario planning affords an excellent way to conduct profound thought experiments and promote the discoveries needed to transform the findings from trend hunting (looking for new ones) and tracking (monitoring the progress of the ones you've already identified) and environmental scanning efforts into clarity about the patterns of change. It also provides a great foundation from which to explore how changes in technology will provoke changes in business models, how new competitors may emerge and potentially alter the structure of the market in significant ways.

Strategies that are then prepared based on the discoveries exposed in a process of scenario planning are likely to have the great virtue of being open-ended rather than deterministic, not overly narrow in their targeting (as we saw with the cone of uncertainty), and fluid rather than fixed. Overall, approaching the future this way provides much better preparation to meet the surprises and challenges lying in wait in an era filled with massive uncertainty.

Thus, scenario planning is both a skill and a valuable tool that helps to foster an effective leadership mindset, while also generating essential insights into specific markets and technologies. These insights will provide important guidance for all stages of the innovation process, including the formulation of new and potentially disruptive business models, as we will see next.

Wide Cone of Uncertainty
Actually, almost anything might happen.

Actual
Wide
Range of
Possible
Futures

A Better
Model

The
Present

time

64

BUSINESS MODEL SHIFT
From Assumed to Designed

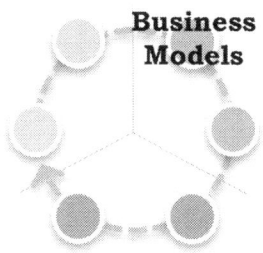

Business Models

INNOVATION

As new technologies come into wide usage they often become forces of disruption, and over time every industry goes through difficult phases of fundamental change as new technologies emerge. During the last few decades we've experienced wave after wave of disruption in retail, financial services, transportation, energy, telecommunications, media, entertainment, etc., etc. No industry has escaped the intense pressures of change, the bankruptcies and takeovers, the downsizings and layoffs, all brought on by digitalization.

And where this change usually impacts most directly is on a firm's or even an entire industry's 'business model.'

The term 'business model' refers both to the way that a firm earns money, and how it is organized to do so. Customers may pay for the work a company does, the products it sells, or the services it provides, and the very structure of the relationship between seller and buyer defines the business model. It is technology that very often changes that structure, and due to the continuing advances of technology we soon realize that all business models are vulnerable.

For example, we used to buy books at a local bookstore until we found that buying them from Amazon is often easier and cheaper. We used to get cash from bank tellers until ATM machines were easier. We used to stand at the curb and wave our arms (in the rain) to hail a taxi until tapping on our smart phones made it so much better to call an Uber or Lyft or Didi.

Another example is Blockbuster Video, which had an immensely successful business model renting movies at its 9000 retail stores. The company dominated the market until Netflix devised a better business model, sending movies via the mail and then later streaming them over the internet. Blockbuster went bankrupt, while Netflix continues to grow and expand.

These are examples of business model disruption, and the key point is that the disruptions aren't finished, they're only getting started. With new waves of new technologies poised to sweep into the market, technologies such as big data, artificial intelligence, robots, ubiquitous sensors, facial recognition, blockchains and cryptocurrencies, genetic engineering and personalized medicine, leaders have to be prepared to recognize that current business models will inevitably become obsolete, while simultaneously engaging in constant exploration for new ways to create compelling experiences for customers.

Part of the challenge they face is that very often the business model of an organization seems so natural that it's an unquestioned assumption. 'This is just how we do things' is the phrase you often hear from those attached to the old ways, and incapable of seeing new threats and possibilities. Often those are some of last words spoken on the way to bankruptcy.

A few years ago I was talking with the leader of a big global firm, and he shared with me that while visiting a shopping mall he had unexpectedly come upon the store of a new competitor. He was surprised to see that the store was organized in a completely different way than his own stores. He said he walked in, looked around, and laughed, knowing that this new business model could never work. 'I was wrong,' he told me sadly, an error that had cost his company billions. He had been unable to recognize that his own assumptions were so deeply hidden that they appeared to him as facts rather than concepts. In his mind, his company's way was the only way.

The lesson is clear: you must expose the assumptions behind your own business model, make them conscious, and then use technology to design better experiences and improved value propositions. That's what your best competitors are doing, that's what the disruptive start-ups are doing, and that's what you must do if you want your company to survive.

And then once you understand the emerging business model landscape, the next step is to develop an equally deep understanding of the technology landscape and how, too, it is likely to impact on your business model.

Blockbuster Video was the undisputed king of the video rental business in the US in 2000. By 2004 it had 9,000 stores that were used by to a huge proportion of Americans.

A small startup company from Silicon Valley called Netflix had a different way to distribute entertainment, and they thought it would make a great complement to Blockbuster's business model. So they offered to sell their company to Blockbuster.

The response?

In the words of Netflix CFO Barry McCarthy 'They just about laughed us out of their office.'

Blockbuster went bankrupt in 2011, while Netflix went on to become one of the most valuable entertainment companies in the world.

65

TECHNOLOGY ROADMAP SHIFT
From Peripheral to Core

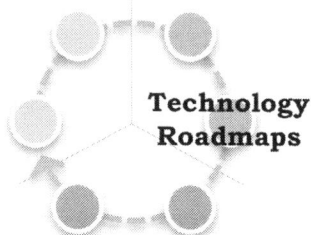

Technology Roadmaps

INNOVATION

Since the amazing usefulness of technology has transformed all markets for all goods and services into technology-based markets, this relentless advance requires that every firm must think of technology as a core element of its business model no matter what else it's doing or making or selling. Consequently, no matter what your business is, it's essential to develop a reliable technology roadmap that defines the direction from the present to the future with a specific focus on the sequence of technologies and technology improvements that will define the success path from today to tomorrow.

This roadmap must address not only the technologies that will be embedded in the products and services that you provide to your customers, but also the technologies that you apply internally in your operations. It's thus a synthesis of everything you know about trends, concepts, scenarios, business models, and the technologies that underlie them.

For example, since computer chips will be used in every product, you need not only a map of trends related to chips, but also the competences required to design and manage the relevant technology applications as they emerge into the market. You also need to collect and manage data in new ways, and to recognize how technology will enable you to manage your own operations in new ways, and what this will require in the way of new competences as well.

Unlike a disruption map (see Section 61), which is intended to be provocative, perhaps a bit disturbing, and rather blue sky in scope, the technology roadmap is a tool for short and medium term decision making and a guide for investment, so short term accuracy is important.

Often the best roadmaps are developed in collaborative settings where it's possible to draw from the expertise of a large number of people, and where they can discuss their differences of opinion to discover and expose differing assumptions and worries. Such discussions inevitably provoke new insights that feed more value back into the planning effort itself.

A good roadmap also provides a very helpful way to track progress on implementation, and even more importantly to monitor the alignment between what's on the map and external events and trends. Inevitably new technologies will emerge that aren't on the map, or that come to market in ways that were unexpected. By comparing the map with evolving reality you can significantly fine tune your alignment with progress in the marketplace, thereby enabling you to more quickly see the emerging patterns and initiate worthwhile responses. Your internal clock speed will thus accelerate in an entirely productive way.

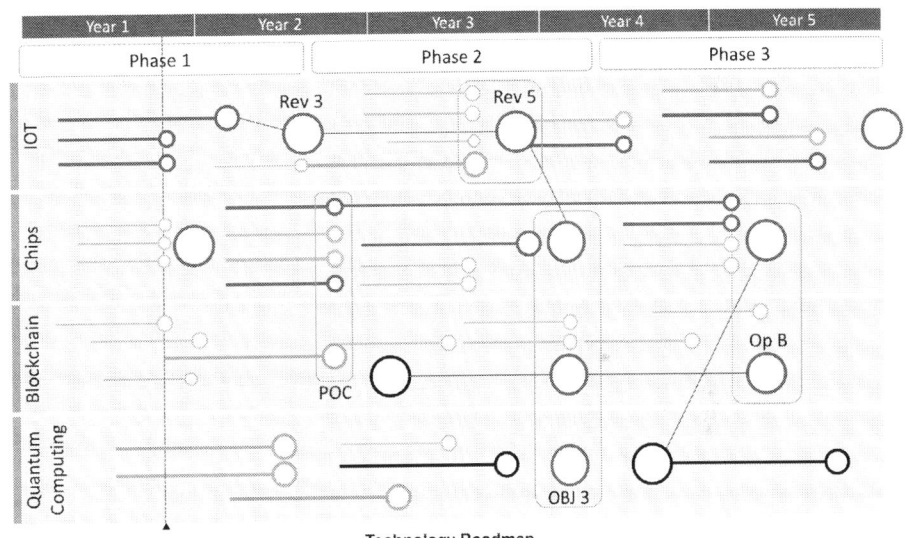

Technology Roadmap

Utilizing your technology roadmap this way, and building upon all the learning you've attained through trend tracking, scenario planning, and business modeling, you're now in the enviable position to create compelling new products and services, for which the invaluable technique called design thinking is ideally suited. Design thinking will enable you to develop a deep understanding of your customers, their behaviors, and their expectations, and so to figure out how you can serve them with new and better experiences.

66

DESIGN THINKING SHIFT
From More to More Compelling

Design Thinking

INNOVATION

In the factories of the industrial economy a person's role was often defined narrowly and experienced as monotony, the endless repetition of the mind-numbing production line. Value was created by repeating one process at scale, so firms grew to massive size by replicating one success across a region and then across dozens, exporting the same products and business models from one nation across entire continents.

But now that the giant global enterprises have achieved global scale and nearly complete saturation of the global market, they're obliged to find a different way. This means that what distinguishes organizations going forward must inevitably shift from 'how to make more' to 'how to make more meaning.' The goal is no longer to produce and sell still more of the same, but to produce differently and better, and in a way that transforms the relationship between company and customer into a partnership.

'Design thinking' is how we gain the knowledge we need do this, a rigorous process that integrates creativity with innovation in the quest for insight into the essential qualities of value.

Design thinking is also a skill, commonly taught and readily learned, such as at Stanford University's 'd' School (where 'd' is for 'design,' of course). d School students learn the techniques of design thinking by practicing it, and their talents are much sought after when they complete their studies. Many of the firms that hire them, of course, are among the leaders in the shift to the new economy, an economy of new business models and originality, where the goal is not more mass but higher quality, and where success is achieved through uniqueness and customization that is attained not just by desire or intent but through better methods and actual skills.

Design thinking is a technique to gain deep insight into customer needs and expectations through *immersion*, the process of exploration and discovery and then mapping the findings. Also referred to as 'tacit knowledge research' and 'ethnographic research,' this approach builds on decades of experiences by ethnographers who traveled the world seeking to understand the hidden nuances of human culture, and who recognized that the most important knowledge is often hidden, or tacit. Only through immersion can we discover the important patterns and make the discoveries that enable us to understand the critical factors of 'use,' 'usability,' and 'meaning:' How is it used, how easy is it to use, and what does it mean to the user? Deep knowledge across all three dimensions provides the essential insights that yield breakthrough products, services, and business models.

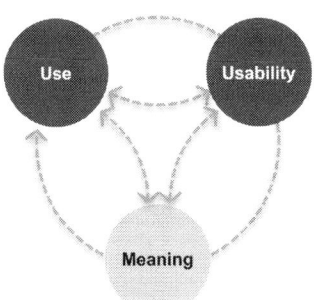

**The 3 Dimensions
Critical to Good Design**
After Beckman and Barry

The diagram below and to the right shows design thinking as a three stage process, and of course this model is already familiar to you because it's exactly the same as the overall model of the full innovation process, but now simply applied at a finer scale. Here we are not strategizing the entire innovation effort, we're creating value at the level of products and projects.

From *immerse* we transition to *invent*, the creation of dozens or even hundreds of possibilities that arise through dialog, exploration, and brainstorming. The best are then refined via *implementation* through rigorous prototyping, user testing, and validation.

These three stages of design thinking constitute a simple but exceptionally effective process that is becoming essential to the creative economy. Billions of dollars of commercial value has already been earned by companies that apply design thinking to guide their product development processes, and hundreds of thousands of lives have been improved and many even saved by applying this powerful approach to address public sector problems in fields including health care, water quality, and decision making.

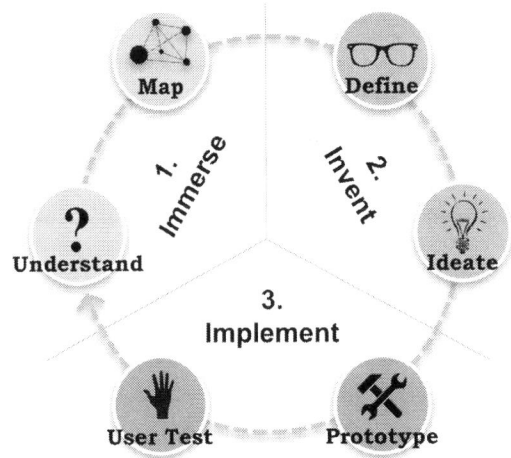

**Design Thinking
For Products, Services, Business Models**
Source: Honey Bajaj
As presented in *The Innovation Formula* by Langdon Morris

Design thinking is a powerful technique for discovering useful knowledge and creating exceptional value for organizations and their customers, and thus a compelling way to organize the 'how,' the essential process of creation in the new economy.

67

INNOVATION MASTERY SHIFT
From Luck to Proficiency

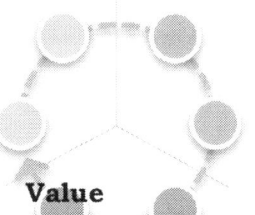

Value Delivery

INNOVATION

There's a lot to be frightened of and worried about, not least the 9 exponential shifts, and all the others as well. But there's also a lot to be excited and enthusiastic about, unlimited possibilities and opportunities that are everywhere, because clearly change is what it's all about. And since someone is going to be making change, it might as well be you.

It's obvious now that something much deeper is going on than just the same basic competitive market dynamics that we've seen for the last 30 years. And since change is inevitable and inexorable, it also means that you can't keep doing the same things and expect to be successful, or even to survive. So while you don't have a choice that change is coming, you have lots of choices about your role in it. Indeed, this is exactly what

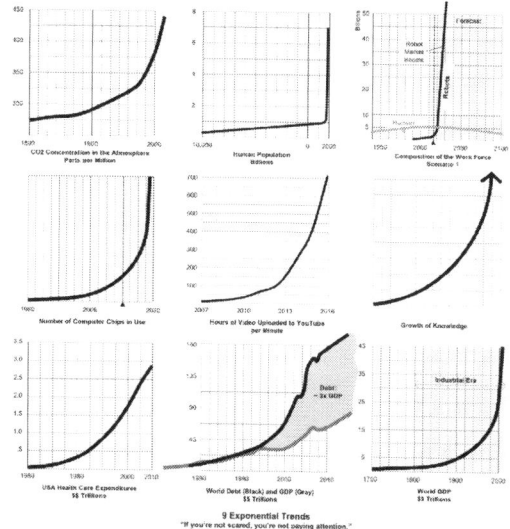

9 Exponential Trends
"If you're not scared, you're not paying attention."

proficiency at innovation gives you, choices, because the pursuit of innovation is really all about the creation of options for the future.

What you cannot wait on is luck. (Remember, the time for innovation is 'now.') You can't assume or expect or hope that someone in your organization is going to come up with some great ideas that will save the day, you must instead be very proactive in learning about and aligning with everything that's changing, and then carefully designing your place in all of it. The tools described on the previous pages and shown to the right can certainly support you, and while you don't need to be dogmatic about the specific sequencing, each of these elements addresses an important aspect of the overall learning process that you'll have to think about in one way or another.

You do have to know why (what's your strategy?), you do have to track the external environment, and you've got to model alternative futures and anticipate where the business model disruptions will likely come from. You've got to craft innovation portfolios that deliver the future to you by engaging with the right amount of risk.

And of course you must have a rigorous process for generating insights and transforming them into value. Again, this isn't about predicting everything about the future, it's about overcoming the many forms of bias that might impede you from recognizing change and responding effectively to it. It's about creating possibilities, which enable you to create future value.

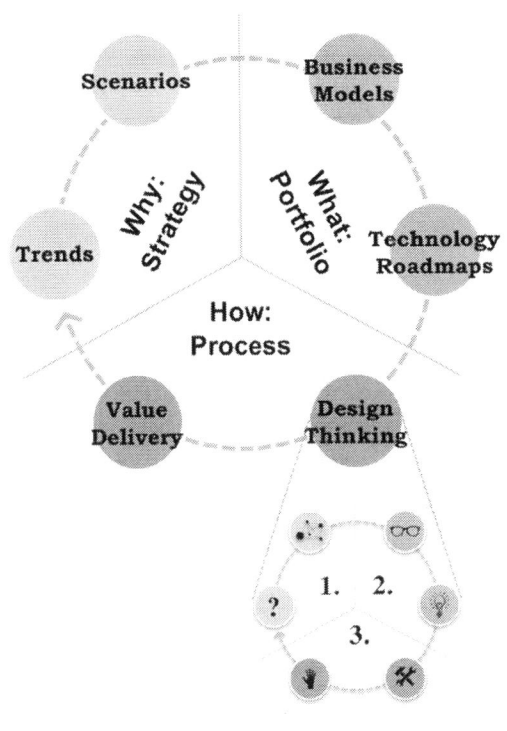

A Rigorous Innovation Planning Framework

New behaviors, new relationships, new connections, new types of transactions, new business models, they're all coming, and fast. In this new world, your new mentality and these new skills will become invaluable.

This all requires, naturally enough, that you look beyond the current quarter, and that you think deeply about the longer term patterns of change. It also requires that you work actively to develop the innovative skills and creative talents throughout your entire organization, and that you actively draw effectively on both.

68

CREATIVE SHIFT
From Optional to Imperative

INNOVATION

Creativity is an attitude that we bring to our lives as well as a skill we bring to our work. We thus describe the 'creative mindset' as the means by which we often achieve the 'creative insight.'

And creative insight is, in turn, the essential foundation for all innovation, for innovation is the essential effort that transforms concepts into value, while insight is where such concepts come from. Thus, while innovation proceeds from the seeds provided by creativity, and indeed it requires creativity, there is no innovation until the initial creative insight actually arrives.

We thus need to distinguish innovation from creativity, which we do by noting that *creativity is the essential process of developing ideas and concepts*, while *innovation is the achievement of new value.* Innovation is the end goal, but creative insight is the essential trigger that enables the often detailed process of transforming insights into products, services, processes, or social benefits to begin.

Thus, the intent of design thinking is precisely to attain such insights, and the three step process model we learned about on the previous pages is our guide.

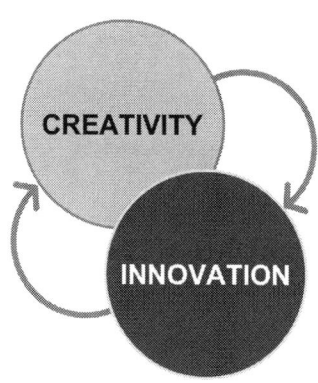

For example, transforming the initial creative sketch of the iPhone (maybe on a napkin) to the fully realized innovative device requires thousands of hours of immersion, ideation, and extensive implementation that requires design, engineering, manufacturing and testing efforts involving hundreds of people (or more), and dozens of organizations.

Further complicating this is the realization that the process and work of developing innovation often leads to new creative insights, for the subsequent steps in the processes of design and engineering, inevitably require *and* inspire lots of creativity as well. Consequently, as creativity leads to innovation, so innovation also leads to creativity. Because the two processes are thus so intimately connected, we think of them as two sides of a single coin.

And since creativity is the launching point from which innovation springs, we readily understand that developing our creative capacities is an essential skill. What we must nurture, then, is our capacity to shift:

- Insight may come from a shift of *perspective*, seeing things in an illuminating new way.

- It may be a shift of *knowledge*, a new capacity to achieve the thing that could not have been done before, because we did not know how.

- It may be a shift of *belief or attitude*, because of which the formerly impossible or unacceptable becomes the given standard, and is thereafter taken for granted.

- It might be a shift of *possibility*, a new tool or technology that transforms the formerly impossible into the suddenly doable.

- It could be a shift of the *market*, newly welcoming a product or service that was previously unknown or unwelcome.

By definition, every innovation marks a shift from the old thing or the old way to the new one, and it's only poetic justice that such a shift originates in the systemic search for shifts that the rigorous innovation process has organized and now achieved.

Thus, as innovation is the essential strategy for dealing with change, and as creativity is the essential the source of innovation, then neither can be considered optional, and both must become strategic imperatives. Change or be changed; disrupt or be disrupted; shift or be shifted; create or be created upon.

Essential to both is the simple characteristic of curiosity.

'We are not used to thinking of ideas as economic goods, but they are surely the most significant ones that we produce. The only way for us to produce more economic value and thereby generate economic growth is to find ever more valuable ways to make use of the objects available to us.'

Paul Romer
The Economist
September 11, 1993

69

CURIOSITY SHIFT
From Acceptance to Quest

INNOVATION

What is it that enables someone to conceive of a great insight that leads to a life-changing, business-changing, or civilization-changing breakthrough? Is it a born talent? Is it a learned skill? Where does it come from?

We've already discussed how design thinking is a technique for generating insights, but even then there's something else. It's a core skill, or perhaps it's better described as an innate quality, and it enables or evokes openness to new possibilities, and indeed a passion for seeking them out. In a word, it's *curiosity*.

Interestingly, curiosity is both born and learned. All children are born with innate curiosity and they experiment relentlessly as they grow, because that is evolution's inbuilt way of motivating us to learn how the world works. Curiosity is the foundation of creativity, for the quest to figure out how it works often leads to the idea that it could work better. As you watch children at play you observe how many experiments they conduct, how many different ways they find to do something, all in a matter of moments.

For many children, however, social pressures and institutionalized education gradually squeeze the curiosity out, leaving them in the lamentable and untrue state of feeling that others are creative, but not them.

The good news is that we can all relearn what we've lost by reawakening our curiosity and developing our willingness and ability to experiment with different viewpoints. Trend tracking (Section 61) is a great way to practice. Challenge yourself and a friend to go on a trend safari, and see how many new behaviors, products, and experiences you can identify. Then map all the trends and see if you can predict some new products or services that may be coming next.

As easy as that, your curiosity may be awakened, and you may find yourself looking at the world differently, and indeed more creatively. As we saw on the previous page, creative breakthroughs both large and small come about due, at root, to a change in perspective or viewpoint of some kind, or more simply, a shift. It may be a shift inside of you, the creator, or it may be a shift outside that you recognize as the harbinger of new possibilities that you wish to exploit. In the previous section I mentioned five shifts, the shifts of *perspective* or of *knowledge*, of *belief or attitude*, of *possibility*, and a shift in the *market*, and the simple trend safari exercise is simply a way to become attuned to these and many other shifts that may be happening all around you.

Once you get started this may become a habit, as one of the most common characteristics shared by creative people is a constant search for new inputs. Driven by curiosity and definitely not satisfied with whatever they know at present, creators study the world around them and do not accept it as it is, but constantly look deeply to see what may be hidden. They see, that is, what others do not see.

Playing with alternatives and possibilities in their minds, in sketchbooks and journals, they seek out new experiences and possibilities rather than the same old ones. Like children, they become natural creators because they are natural questioners. They raise ideas and questions with colleagues, engage in the endless process of 'what if,' and 'suppose,' and always, of course, asking 'why.'

Thus, children seek to understand the world by experimenting with it, and creative adults do exactly the same thing. The library of creativity resources is immense and inspiring. Determine to be or become a creator, study, practice, and allow your innate curiosity to lead you on your own magnificent quest.

And along the way, don't be afraid to fail.

70

FAILURE SHIFT
From Fear of Failure to Getting it Right

INNOVATION

If innovation was easy to accomplish then we wouldn't need to talk about it much because everyone would just be out doing it. But it is difficult, and consequently those who do it really well often become celebrities. Millions want to know the secrets of Steve Jobs, Bill Gates, and Warren Buffet, or how history's great innovators such as Einstein, da Vinci, Edison, Napoleon, Tesla, Galileo, and Newton made their great breakthroughs.

What do they all have in common? What makes an innovative genius? Hard work, certainly. Edison called innovation '10% inspiration, and 90% perspiration.' Being in the right place time at the right time also matters, as reflected in Pasteur's comment that 'luck favors the prepared mind.' I believe that what he meant is that you make your own luck, which Golfer Gary Player once expressed in commenting that 'the more I practice, the luckier I get.'

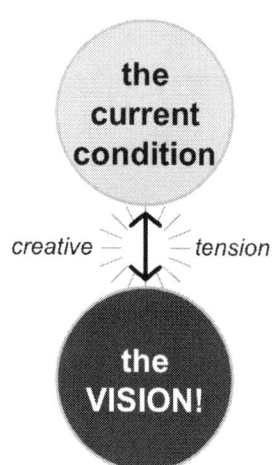

As I noted above, curiosity is definitely part of it, the desire to know how the world works and how to make the things that you want to work, work better.

Dissatisfaction is also common among innovators. In the mind's eye the innovator sees the possibility of a better way, and the contrast between what's in the mind and what's in the hand is a powerful motivator that drives both the curiosity-driven exploration and the creative making and testing of concepts and models. The contrast between the envisioned ideal, the vision, and inadequate reality, the current condition evokes the nagging feeling called 'creative tension,' a sense of urgency that compels innovators forward even when the going is tough and the path is not at all clear.

The willingness to try new things and to fail without

becoming distraught is also characteristic of innovators. Indeed, failure is inescapable in the innovation process, and those who cannot endure its pain don't generally stay engaged. We can express it this way: we call it 'innovation' precisely because we *don't know* how to do it. If we did know, we'd call it something else, like 'engineering.' But since we don't know, we have to try many possibilities and assuredly they won't all work. Hence, the pursuit of innovation always brings the possibility of failure. And if we get disturbed or disappointed by failure so much so that we lose our drive, then this tells us that the nature of the innovation quest may not be for us.

Thomas Edison once noted in regard to the development of the light bulb that although his team had failed hundreds of times to identify the most suitable filament material, this long string of failures didn't deter them. It simply meant that they would have to try 'something else.' There was no stigma or drama in this, as each 'failure' was simply further accumulation of useful knowledge, and so another step forward on the journey to the eventual solution.

And of course uncertainty is inexorably embedded in this process, as the journey's end point is not known when you take the first step. It may take weeks, months, even years, or you may never reach the destination at all; such is the risk. Hence, those who are not comfortable with ambiguity and uncertainty also struggle as innovators, while those who use uncertainty as a source of motivation and who tolerate living with ambiguity while working to eliminate it are usually the ones who become innovation icons.

Innovation and the necessity of failure are as pertinent for organizations as for individuals. Companies that do it well tend to far out-perform their less innovative competitors. And so while we appreciate Apple's many great innovations, we also should not forget its many failures. It had dozens of products that flopped in the market, some quite spectacularly, the history of which demonstrate the continual quest to get it right. That they provided immensely valuable knowledge which enabled the company to eventually get it exactly right is certain.

'Creative individuals do not rush to define the nature of problems; they look at the situation from various angles first and leave the formulation undetermined for a long time. They consider different causes and reasons. They test their hunches about what really is going on, first in their own mind and then in reality.

They try tentative solutions and check their success – and they are open to reformulating the problem if the evidence suggests they started out on the wrong path.'

Mihaly Csikszentmihalyi
Creativity: Flow and the Psychology of Discovery and Invention

'I've missed more than 9,000 shots in my career. I've lost almost 300 games. 26 times, I've been trusted to take the game-winning shot and missed. I've failed over and over and over again in my life. And that is why I succeed.'

Michael Jordan

'You have to be able to accept failure to get better.'

LeBron James

71

SKILL SHIFT
MAKERS

Innovation is a fascinating topic, and also a complex one. From a cultural and historical perspective the term 'innovation' describes the force that created civilization, and continues to push it forward. We do things differently now, we live differently, and think differently, because of countless innovations that our predecessors made, and the wide ranging impacts these have had on our actions and lifestyles as well as on our beliefs, attitudes, and expectations. History is accelerating all around us as more changes arrive faster and faster, and innovation is behind nearly all of it.

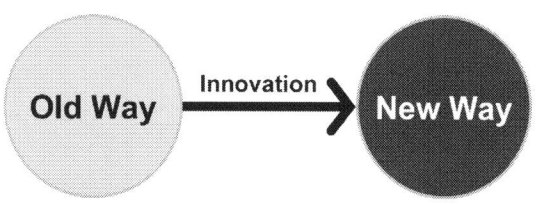

From a business perspective it's obvious that innovation is the essential driver of both marketplace competition and overall economic progress, the driver from old way to new way. Individual companies depend on innovation to remain in business, and they study innovations introduced by competitors because innovation so often yields valuable advantage. To lag at innovation is to fall behind, perhaps disastrously.

The economy as a whole progresses as the aggregate of innovation across all firms and governments, which can be messy and destructive as some firms are pushed aside to die painfully as new ones come forward with new ideas, new innovations, thereby creating the shifts we experience. Economist Joseph Schumpeter astutely labeled this endless cycle of capitalism 'creative destruction,' as old ideas, products, and markets are shoved aside, and the firms that cannot adapt quickly enough also die out in a continual process of renewal.

For society as a whole the process of creative destruction is the definition of progress, but for the individuals directly affected the destructive side of creative destruction can be traumatic and devastating.

Despite the costs, the train of progress shows no signs of stopping, and so all firms must develop the twin capabilities of creativity and innovation to survive. As such, creativity and innovation are no longer optional, they're mandatory.

•••

The core process of value creation in any economic era also provides its name, and so it will be in the next economy as well. As the industrial economy transitions into the digital economy, the essence of value creation necessarily shifts from 'making more things' to 'conceiving of better ideas.' The ideas themselves alone are not sufficient, however, as it's essential to know what to do with ideas, that is, how to turn brilliantly creative insights into landmark innovations. This is a systematic shift of skills across all facets of 'making' and 'creating.'

Interestingly, the shift to the digital has two distinct but related drivers. First is technology itself, and soon the prevalence of robots, which will willingly perform countless cycles of repetitive work without complaints, breaks, or meals, thereby rendering humans progressively redundant and unnecessary in the core activities of production. Machines will do the heavy work and almost all manual tasks so they, not people, will be the essential makers.

The second driver is a result of robotization. It will leave humans to focus on insights, ideas, and inventions, on solving the wicked problems and creating unique outputs that come from abstract, high-level tasks like conceiving, problem-spotting, discovering, exploring, thinking, reasoning, and ideating. That is, humans will create value not by making more stuff, but through our unique capacity to discover and create ideas and insights and innovations that make the world better.

'It takes skill to bring something you imagined into the world: to use words to create believable lives, to select the colors and textures of paint to represent a haystack at sunset, to combine ingredients to make a flavorful dish.

No one is born with that skill. It is developed through exercise, through repetition, through a blend of learning and reflection that's both painstaking and rewarding. And it takes time.

Even Mozart, with all his innate gifts, needed to get twenty-four youthful symphonies under his belt before he composed something enduring with number twenty-five.

If art is the bridge between what you see in your mind and what the world sees, then skill is how you build that bridge.'

Twyla Tharp
The Creative Habit

CONCLUSION
The New Map
And the Macro Disruptors

Through Parts 1, 2, and 3 I've described 70 of the most significant shifts occurring right now all across our global society. There may be others that I could discuss, and perhaps some very important ones, but in any case I hope that the message is clear: you can't keep doing things the same way you've been doing them for the past years or decades. Society has reached the turning point to Phase 3, and to succeed tomorrow you've got to shift your mindset and develop new skills.

Perhaps a useful way to express this is to suggest that we've got to create a new map, because the old ones aren't accurate any more.

Interestingly, the actual world map that we've been using for the last 500 years or so is also woefully inaccurate. The Mercator projection, as it's known, was created in 1569 to serve the needs of European sailors as they ventured westward to the New World, and southward around Africa. It suffers from two significant distortions.

First, Mercator drew the Earth as though it were a cylinder rather than a sphere, so the further from the equator you look, the more distorted the image becomes. Greenland appears on the Mercator map to be many times larger than Australia although in fact the reverse is true; Australia has about 4 times more land area. If you plan a trip based on this map you may be in for unpleasant surprises.

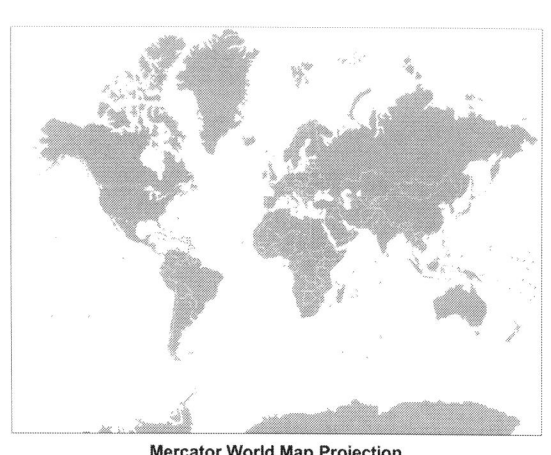

Mercator World Map Projection
Highly Distorted
(Source: Wikimedia, Geordie Bosanko)

The other major distortion is that Europe is placed in the very center and on top. In space, which is where the Earth

156

rotates, there is no 'up' or 'down,' and any alien who happens to be zipping past in a UFO could well see Antarctica or Chile at the 'center' from the perspective of their passing ship. This is problematic because 'above,' 'on top,' and 'at the center' all have potentially divisive social meanings in human culture, and so showing the map as Mercator has done brings forth social assumptions that carry distortion-creating nuances.

The point is that as 2020 rapidly approaches, we have to be prepared to adopt a new mindset and to create new and better maps. The quality of our future matters not upon what land mass or culture is at the center, but very much on our capacity to correctly model and thereby understand the rapidly changing realities of our world, and to create change that adds value and meaning to our lives.

What, then, should our map show? Certainly we should expect turbulence and confusion, danger and discord, upheaval and revolution, reaction and counterrevolution. We have them already. We know that new waves of technology are steadily advancing, that climate and cities and energy systems are in flux, and that many are at serious risk, but that great opportunities exist as well. We experience demagogues and authoritarians exploiting the growing fear and uncertainty, for with the arrival of paradigm change come ardent defenders of the old who promote a return to the old ways, no matter how counterproductive their means or their message.

What else should we expect?

On the following pages I propose some suppositions, the purpose of which is not so much to be right about the future, but because while it's fun to be right, it's important, prudent, and useful to consider what *could* happen. The act of thinking through a prediction requires one to think about possibilities, about what should happen, and especially about the world we wish to create.

What follows then are some thought experiments, ten notions about what might happen if the disruptions turn out to be really, *really* big, and mostly really bad.

DISRUPTORS ▶ **72**

ECONOMIC DISRUPTION
Post Industrial Economics

The transition out of the industrial economy is already happening. As I've noted, this isn't primarily because of the failure of industrialism, but rather because of its tremendous successes. Its terminal condition is brought about both from within by its own creations, such as advanced robotics and urbanized populations in super-massive cities, and from without by factors including climate change and resource shortages that are also the industrial economy's outcomes.

So what happens next? That's the big question, isn't it!

Logic gives us some elements of the answer. The mechanism of capitalism that concentrates ever more power and wealth in the hands of ever fewer people is probably not sustainable, nor is a level of indebtedness that's many times greater than the combined productive capacity of everyone together. Industrial capitalism has seen crises induced by these factors before, in the 1870s and 1930s, and in both cases the underlying conditions were rampant financial speculation accompanied by ballooning debts. This suggests that a reckoning is therefore coming, but whether this is going to result in a reset of the basic capitalist model or a shift to something quite different isn't presently knowable. Either way, it's not going to be much fun.

But there are also wonderful possibilities and prospects, for a system awash in free capital as ours presently is can take on and tackle huge challenges, reinventing enormous stretches of our physical landscapes and our cultural understandings. We can, that is, reinvent ourselves.

73

ROBOT DISRUPTION
Post Human Civilization

The essential story of industrialism has been the progressive substitution of machine power for animal and human muscle, the substitution of capital for labor. While often sold as 'labor-saving' and as ways to make life easier, the parallel consequence has been constant shifting in the structure of labor demand. But now robots have the potential to eliminate demand for labor altogether.

So when we think about what robotics could bring we'll not make the mistake of thinking, 'What's the worst that could happen?' as if it was going to be a minor blip in the otherwise perfect flow of good times. No, clearly the most highly disruptive state that the robotic revolution could result in will be the total destruction of life as we know it, the shift to a way of living that none of us would choose.

Certainly change will not stop with robots, as conversely it will most likely accelerate. Is the majority of humanity therefore headed for mass unemployment and destitution? Or will there still be jobs for people to do? Or conversely, will the structure of the economy change such that the distribution of wealth is no longer linked to 'doing a job' or 'earning a salary?'

And looking forward to the 2040s and the potential arrival of the singularity, with robot intelligence that exceeds human capacities by orders of magnitude, what sort of a society would we live in then?

These are provocative questions for which we have no answers. The answers we can be sure of are that robots are coming, that they will be disruptive, and thus we should be prepared for the unexpected.

74

GEOPOLITICS DISRUPTION
Imbalances of Power

The nation-state system that dates to 1648 (see Section 29) has lasted for 370 years because nations have understood that a balance of power is better than the alternative of constant warfare. While they have competing aims, now that economic strength is understood to be the primary determinant of every nation's well-being, balance is better for business. The balance does shift periodically due to a variety of forces, such as economics, nationalism, ideology, opportunism, the arms race, and imperial ambition, but for three centuries it has endured.

The Big Shift now threatens this balance, as a combination of forces drive the growth and development of powerful and highly disruptive forces that exist beyond the boundaries of the state. Climate change threatens to annihilate the small, low-lying nations entirely, while simultaneously putting severe pressure on coastal cities and turning productive farms into wastelands and deserts. It is certainly a powerful force of *dis*integration.

And there are other forces acting the same way. Many applications of digital technology threaten the primacy of the sovereigns, among them the cryptocurrencies that are specifically designed to replace state-issued currencies with forms of money protected by encryption and defined by consensus rather than governmental fiat. Social media can be a significant disrupter, as we saw with the 2011 Arab Spring uprisings that were largely self-organized via Twitter and Facebook. It is not by accident that all social media are closely monitored in all authoritarian countries, and digital surveillance is now accepted as a fact of life everywhere.

Criminal gangs and terrorists degrade sovereignty as well, and we can easily envision how all these forces of imbalance and disintegration may converge in a way that renders the nation-state progressively irrelevant. And then there are those robots, and will they recognize any sense of national identity?

75

CLIMATE DISRUPTION
Civilization in Crisis

Climate scientists are nearly unanimous in their assessment that human activity causes global climate change, and that climate change is going to create monumental problems for human society. What we do not yet know is how bad it will become, or how soon the bad times will arrive.

DISRUPTOR

But there is already short term suffering. The civil war annihilating Syria may have been caused by and certainly has been worsened by prolonged drought that scientists attribute to climate change. Farmers were forced off the land and into cities when the rains failed, and the resulting crowding and social stresses contributed to the self-destructive social climate.

Meanwhile, every year brings new reports of melting glaciers and sea level rise that already threaten some low-lying coastal locations. All of this will only worsen, and the worst case outcomes pose a major threat to the poorest and vulnerable populations who already lack food security, and who will experience chronic water shortages that will force mass migrations. Millions will be victims, stateless and crowded into desperate refugee camps, lives in continual crisis. Rapidly rising oceans will flood coastal cities rendering trillions of dollars of what was once highly valued ocean-front real estate worthless. As all that wealth is submerged, huge mortgages defaults and massive insurance losses will swamp the financial sector causing a massive crisis that would dwarf the collapse of 2008.

Climate change thus has the makings of a genuine crisis across all of human civilization. It might not be that bad, and we might address it proactively, but we might not and so far we've not done well. Certainly under all but the most benign outcomes, the economic consequences will change the structures of economic life at a most fundamental level.

76

URBAN DISRUPTION
New Cities Beyond Squalor

DISRUPTOR Migration into the cities will most likely continue during the coming decades until just about everyone is a city dweller, ballooning the world's urban population to perhaps 7 billion or more. Most of these urbanites, especially the later arrivals, will not be living in comfortable urban high-rise towers, nor in gracious homes in the suburbs. Instead they'll be crammed into progressively worse slums and favelas surrounding the world's business centers, most lacking clean water, sewage, or stable employment. Still they will come, because the alternatives in the countryside are worse.

Many cities will become impossibly massive, 40 or 50 million crowded in, all searching for a better life. Birthrates will drop, and so the population explosion will switch to implosion. How this is all going to work out remains to be seen, to be created that is, because these cities will be vibrant and full of culture and opportunity, but also full of congestion, disease, crime, and despair.

Climate change further complicates this story because of the possibility of massive coastal flooding and the consequent displacement of billions. But in this also lies an intriguing possibility, the option to build new cities on higher ground. They could be designed differently than today's cities, eco-cities, pedestrian friendly, energy efficient, equitable, clean and safe, enriching lives rather than enabling fraudulent lifestyles of excess consumption.

The dream of the new city is as old as civilization, of course, and through the centuries, generations of visionaries have drawn up plans for life among gleaming towers and lovely gardens. Perhaps in this century some of these visions will become reality, thereby achieving a disruption that makes things much better rather than much worse.

77

BLOCKCHAIN DISRUPTION
Post-Money Money

There is no shortage of demons in economic theory, or in daily economic life. Inflation can ravage a nation's currency, bringing despair and social breakdown, while deflation can bring productive activity to a sputtering halt, idling the engines of economic creativity. A run on the banks, a credit squeeze, labor shortages or excesses, bureaucracy, kleptocracy and corruption, it seems that the entire economic system consists of opportunities for breakdown. And then there's that debt bomb thing, sure to go off, but when? Perhaps the miracle of the economy is that it works at all.

That it does work reasonably well is largely because the system is inherently adaptable, driven by personal ambition and individual choices, bringing each day new possibilities and opportunities. Individuals set the course, informed or misinformed as the case may be, but in any case not predetermined or dictated.

As we enter the digital era, the economy's capacity to adapt will be well exercised, for the digital world brings many fundamental changes to the micro and macro structures of economic life. Robots, of course, change nearly everything about the process of production, and cryptocurrencies could alter how we exchange value, replacing money and government oversight with self-organizing mechanisms that are based on consensus rather than the power of the state.

In their full expression, blockchain-based currencies will result in widespread social change, although for better or worse it's impossible to tell. They could lead to even more economic bifurcation, the few ultra-rich become even richer while the many everyone else slide further back. But they could also become forces of balance and equity that counteract the regressive nature of a debt-based economy and foster both hope and meaningful opportunity.

DISRUPTOR

78

USA DISRUPTION
Post Partisan

DISRUPTOR The high drama of today's American politics reflects a culture that holds two deeply contrasting visions of both its purpose and its future. Left and right, red and blue, liberal and conservative are facile labels for more complex realities, but the nature of two party governance has resulted in a system that is now entirely characterized by oversimplification. Highly complex and nuanced issues are reduced to tweets, insinuations, claims, and counter-claims.

Whereas American political leaders in many eras understood that their responsibility was to reach agreements on behalf of the American people, the nature of politics has shifted to a partisan war for domination, in which compromise is widely interpreted as failure. This shift reflects a tribal mentality in which those on each side support the members of their own tribe regardless of the issues at hand or the realities under discussion, and in which attacks on character have replaced discussions of substance.

As the issues and challenges that must be addressed become more difficult and more complex, the incapacity of America's political leaders to agree on the basics of effective and necessary governance and decision making creates significant risks for American society. Where this all leads is an intriguing mystery, as it's too early to know if we're witnessing the terminal decline of a once-powerful nation, or merely a low point from which America will nicely rebound. A worst-case scenario suggests that the current jokes about various states wishing to secede from the union will turn serious, but as the composition of the overall American populace continues to shift, political power will shift along with it, and it's possible that a new, post-partisan consensus could emerge.

Under any scenario, the coming decades are certain to be turbulent and highly contentious.

79

WARFARE DISRUPTION
Revenge of the Killbots

Digital technology brings with it many amazing possibilities and benefits, but also many new and frightening ways to create death and destruction, not least of which are killer robots (killbots), entire armies consisting only of robots, engineered viruses and diseases, and digital attacks on the essential infrastructures of modern society.

DISRUPTOR

Drones are already common above the battlefield, as we saw more than 500 drone strikes unleashed in the Middle East and Western Asia during President Obama's eight years in office. Terrorist organizations have now developed their own drones and also used commercial ones right out of the box to launch deadly attacks.

Now these capabilities are being deployed *on* the battlefield, with robotic soldiers soon to accompany or even replace human ones altogether, bringing with them enhanced lethal capabilities but reduced ethical sensitivities, a brutal combination that has many people deeply worried. In addition to the obvious factors of size, mobility, and deadly weaponry, the robotic battlefield is one of speed. As *The Economist* puts it (April 28, 2018), 'The generals know they are entering an era in which algorithms will determine success on the battlefield, and humans may be unable to keep up with the pace of combat.'

It has largely been due to self restraint that the world has avoided a nuclear confrontation, but during the Cold War period the logic of deterrence led to the development of some very bizarre notions, such as the doctrine of Mutually Assured Destruction, and its entirely suitable acronym of MAD. Neither self-restraint nor deterrence are likely to be at the forefront when robots battle robots, even though civilians are sure to be caught in the middle, and the destruction will encompass all aspects of the human habitat.

The potential for the utter disruption of social norms and conventions is frighteningly close at hand.

80

SPACE DISRUPTION
Post-Earth Civilization

DISRUPTOR The Space Age began half a century ago with the promise of commerce and civilization spreading into the frontier of space, and while progress has been slow, today's satellite industry is already a $270 billion dollar annual business that produces enormous knowledge and financial benefits. But large scale habitation of space remains elusive, and so the question remains as to whether we really will migrate to space, or if it will remain merely a fantasy.

Certainly there's no shortage of entrepreneurs chasing that dream, but will they succeed, or merely squander their incredible fortunes?

If they do succeed, then when the number of off-Earth inhabitants attains meaningful scale this fact will necessarily transform human culture and surely the economy as well. The entire political situation will alter when off-Earth colonies become meaningful political entities, and while this is not going to happen soon, it's a fascinating prospect to consider. Will your own grandchildren migrate to live on another world, or on an orbiting space station, never to return? Or will they just have a fun-filled honeymoon in an orbiting hotel and then return to a normal, Earth-bound life?

And how quickly will off-Earth inhabitants evolve into new species or sub-species, fully adapted to their new living arrangements? Naturally they will develop and apply advanced capabilities in biotechnology to both enhance their survival odds and exploit their new environments. Consequently, new sub-specialties in biotechnology and genetics will arise, such as 'zero-g adaptation' and 'cosmic radiation resistance,' among others.

Science in space will also advance rapidly, and with the innate characteristics of micro-gravity environments we will see new waves of innovation and even entirely new scientific paradigms emerge. In all respects, civilization will be fundamentally changed.

81

WILDCARD DISRUPTIONS
Civilization Collapsers

On the previous pages I've highlighted possible disruptions that the coming years and decades may bring, disruptions that are visible because they result from trends and possibilities that we can already see coming. There are others that I've not mentioned which also should be included for the sake of compiling a more complete list of what might go massively wrong.

- If a major, world-scale war was to break out then it would immediately change everything, because today's weapons are so powerful that the scale of destruction would be immense and so the whole thing would be so quickly. The end of civilization is entirely imaginable, even without nuclear weapons.

- Detonation of a nuclear device, whether by a nation or a terror organization, would be massively destructive and psychologically debilitating, and a nuclear or chemical war would bring the present era of civilization to an abrupt and definitive close.

- Other wildcard threats include massive viral pandemics either naturally evolved such as the Black Plague or engineered as genetic weaponry; a large meteor strike such as the one that wiped out the dinosaurs; or climate change so far beyond worst case that famine and destruction occur on a global scale.

- If the global debt bomb explodes and all trust is lost, then the collapse of the financial sector is easy to foresee, effectively wiping out the global economy and leaving only local markets.

Under all these worst-case wildcards the magnitude of the upheaval and fear sets the stage for the rise of strong-arm dictatorships, demagogues, and juntas that promise to bring order amid widespread social and political chaos.

While none of these catastrophes are inevitable, all are possible. Such is life in our period of fundamental and accelerating change and rampant uncertainty.

82

REMEDIES SHIFT
Aspirations and Inspirations

Short of collapse, the transition from industrialism to the digital economy seems to be unstoppable, so whether we want it or not, it's apparently arriving very soon, along with all the other changes that come with it.

These include the many shifts and disruptions I've described on the previous pages, but also an entire universe of great possibilities and wonderful opportunities.

Because in spite of the huge momentum of change, it's important to remember that we still do have choice. And we also have the tools, now, to seize those best possibilities and opportunities, to make them real, and perhaps we even have the skill and wisdom to evade or avoid the worst of the negative outcomes, or at least to respond appropriately to them.

And so as we think about what we will create and how we will do it, we must ask this important question, *What is the purpose of our system?*

The industrial model has demonstrated its power to transform human life for better, which it does by transforming raw materials and human creativity into food and medicine, health care and shelter and entertainment, joy and knowledge and comfort.

But industrialism can also make things much worse. It has taught us that it makes no sense to optimize social and economic systems solely to enable capital to create more capital, to make the wealthy even richer, when that necessarily leads to the destruction of the environment upon which we depend, and to the degradation of human beings, of ourselves. Both have been prominent outcomes of industrial capitalism.

And so when our answer to the question is that the purpose of the system is to make the whole better, and not just some of the parts, then we have the necessary context for productive change, and a set of goals toward which the emergence of the digital economy must be directed. The purpose must be to serve humans, not just wealthy humans, which gives us a basis for useful and meaningful choices and actions.

The digital economy could indeed harness industrialism's might in even more positively powerful and transformative ways, just as industrialism has so harnessed the agriculture that came before it, and so we must be prepared to direct this power thoughtfully. Digital technologies are proficient means for enabling and promoting creativity, and will certainly lead to new forms of expression and also new ways of giving in service. They can lead to exceptional connectivity and collaboration, cooperation and problem solving.

Attaining these positive outcomes will require in particular the skills of leadership and systems design and innovation, and the commitment to learning and coaching and teams. These concepts and principles we can apply to prolong and enhance our organizations and communities, turning toward that which makes us better, and away from that which drags us toward our lesser selves.

These are our remedies, the principles that lead toward the fulfillment of our aspirations and our inspirations.

83

WHAT DOESN'T SHIFT
Human Values

Technology, markets, economies, cultures, attitudes, business models, etc., etc., they're all shifting. After all this talk about the Big Shift and the dozens of contributing shifts that are driving us with such inexorable momentum, the question naturally arises as to what in this new world *doesn't* shift.

That is, will this new world require us also to discard what we revere as the essential human qualities? Do empathy, compassion, appreciation, and love change, or may they all remain as we know them today? Will we change our ways of appreciating great beauty throughout the arts and sciences, the joys of painting and sculpture, architecture, dance and music, mathematics and biology, chemistry and physics?

New forms of art will emerge in a society suffused with an abundance of new tools, technologies, and toys, but aesthetics need not change, unless we wish them to. Michelangelo and Mozart, Beethoven and Shakespeare, Hadid and Baryshnikov may remain in the pantheon of our highest esteem.

But perhaps it is our sense of ethics and justice that needs to change. Or is fairness still fairness? This is no longer a trivial question, not in an era of the 1% rich and the 99% everyone else; in an era facing the prospect of possibly millions of climate refugees; in an era when merely being born a Syrian or Sudanese is likely the delivery into a life of misery; in an era when the holder of an American or EU passport can travel the world freely, but the holder of an African passport has no such freedoms, and the holder of no passport is likely trapped in one of the dozens of despondent refugee camps that sprawl across the wasteland deserts of North Africa and the Middle East, with no means of exit.

If we choose to acknowledge this as a basic unfairness and work to overcome it then we may say that our sense of ethics is consistent with human aspirations across centuries, but if instead we say, 'Too bad for you,' then what does that say about us?

Ethics will soon face another challenging question, for it's apparent that in the not distant future we will be confronted with fundamental issues related to the rights of people displaced by robots, and perhaps the rights of robots displaced by people. How do we define 'consciousness,' and how do we determine if a robot is indeed conscious? Can a silicon device be 'alive?' Today we do not know the answers to these questions, but when (and if) the singularity does indeed arrive, then we will be obliged to reconsider our definition of consciousness, and similarly of the meanings of terms like 'rights' and 'justice.'

And if robots do achieve the consciousness-singularity threshold then human-machine hybrids will arrive with them. Already we are becoming hybrids with artificial joints and limbs, with neuro implants and exoskeletons. Would the rights enjoyed by a human-machine hybrid be the same as the rights accorded to a human? Is a 50-50 hybrid a robot, or a human? Would a robot, if determined to be self-conscious, have the 'right' to the electrical power needed to sustain its circuits in operating order? Will it have the right to freedom? Will it have the right to vote, and run for political office? Will we properly call it 'it,' or something else?

Yesterday these were questions in science fiction; by tomorrow morning they will be pressing questions in ethics, law, politics, and also in economics.

Thus, when we ask 'What doesn't shift?' we're really inquiring into the depths and meanings of our own humanness, which brings into question why it is that we have an economy at all, and why we create change, and what are the ends toward which our society and its economy are directed.

The point of having an economy is to meet needs, and perhaps to make a few people rich along the way. But as our responsibilities to one another endure while our pleasures are ephemeral, we can be sure that the point of having a civilization is to accomplish great things. We can make civilization and the world better, and through the opportunity presented by the Big Shift this is what we should do.

POSTSCRIPT

The challenge I set out to address when I started writing this book was to communicate a complex story in a way that was clear and preferably compelling, and that would empower young people and indeed any reader to see the world as it really is and is becoming, and so to help them align their choices and intentions with the emerging future rather than becoming attached to the fading past.

Through the course of the many fascinating dialogs that led to this book we explored when a golf cart is no longer a golf cart (often), when a revolution provokes a counter-revolution (nearly always), when a car is a computer (always, in today's world), how and when a map can lie (easily, and often), what creates a martyr, how an army becomes ineffective in the face of a popular uprising, and of course my main topic here, what the world's next economy is going to be like for us, our children, and grandchildren.

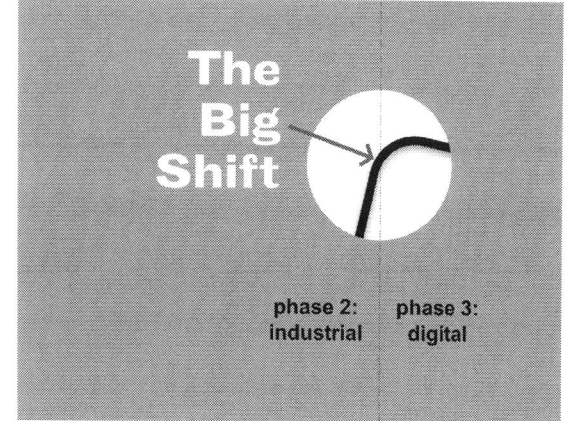

The Big Shift

phase 2: industrial   phase 3: digital

These are important questions about important topics, but they're also Zen-like paradoxes that arise when we attempt to grasp concepts that have a different structure, and when we try to comprehend a future that has not yet fully arrived. They engage us in problems of perception and expectation, mindset and pattern recognition, forecasting and hoping.

And these, indeed, are the problems that we all face when we think about the future. We wonder what it has in store for us. And we wonder how we may empower our young people, our leaders, and indeed all of us to bring forth the qualities and characteristics and experiences to make the world better, safer, happier, and more secure. How may we live more joyously and contribute to the world's well-being more fully?

These many shifts are occurring across many fields of study, including technology, the climate, our cities and countryside, while the Big Shift is the aggregate of all the smaller ones (although none of them are really small), which I take to be the emergence of an entirely new operating model for the world economy.

That a new model is emerging is little doubted; what its eventual form and characteristics will be is still very much in doubt, for it's really just too soon to tell what's going to happen. We have clues, certainly, and some elements of that economy are coming more clearly into focus, but still vast reaches are beyond our ability to accurately foresee.

Nevertheless, it's important to look in the future, hazy or not, and I've done my best to explain it here, and to describe how we may in Phase 3 aspire to and create greatness across all of human civilization, moving beyond stuff to meaning, beyond mass to intelligence, and beyond 'more for me' to 'better for everyone,' in all that this involves and demands.

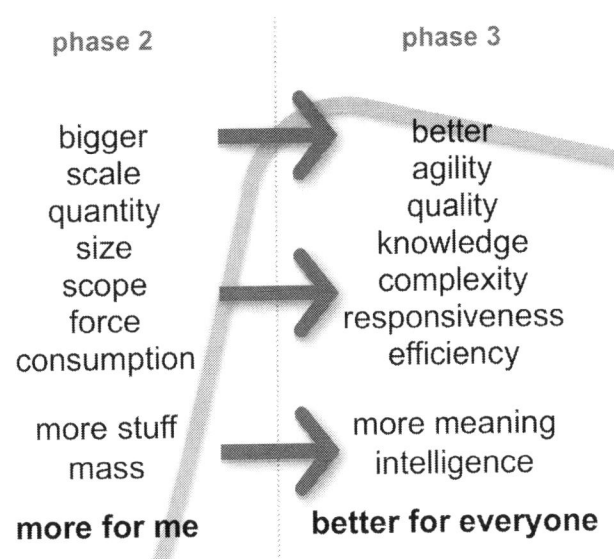

GLOSSARY OF THE FUTURE

Language evolves as society evolves, and since our society is evolving at a furious pace, new words are being created every day to label new experiences, new knowledge, and new stuff. It takes some effort just to keep up, and thus the purpose of this glossary is to offer a useful list of words and concepts that I've used in the book and which relate to topics covered in the book, and which newly describe essential and essentially new aspects of today's world, and which may also describe tomorrow's. It's not a complete list, but many of the 140 concepts are ones you probably hadn't heard of not so long ago (because they hadn't been invented yet), but which may turn out to be key descriptors of tomorrow.

For additional concepts and their descriptions, please visit the very insightful site, "The Bureau of Linguistical Reality" at bureauoflinguisticalreality.com

A previous version of this glossary appeared in *Foresight and Extreme Creativity*.

Additive Manufacturing – Machines that create new stuff in layers, by adding. More complex shapes and forms can be made this way. Printers can be located anywhere – on the Space Station, in your kitchen, etc. Additive manufacturing removes the factory from the factory. Also known as 3D printing. The "MakerBot" company is popularizing these machines, and an MakerBot at the San Francisco Public Library is being used to produce customized artificial limbs for amputees at a small fraction of the previous cost. (See Section 62: *3D Shift*)

Agglomeration Economy – Economic gains including higher output per worker, higher wages, higher profits, and higher incomes that come from concentration of firms and people, typically as they congregate in cities. London and Silicon Valley are prime examples, as both show significant concentrations of expertise, wealth creation, and higher incomes than neighboring cities and regions. (Mario Polèse, *The Wealth & Poverty of Regions*, p. 31)

Anti-Fragile – Technically, anti-fragile is something that becomes stronger when it is stressed, as distinct from fragile, which breaks when it is stressed. (Nassim Nicolas Taleb, *Anti-Fragile*. Random House, 2012)

Autocatalytic – Literally, something that produces the fuel that propels it; in our context, a process of change that feeds itself such that further change results. (Henrich, p. 57) In the urban context, on a street where interesting things happen, more interesting things then happen. (Charles Montgomery, *Happy City*, p. 151) (See also, *Autopoesis*.)

Autopoesis, Self-creation – A process that creates itself. Similar to autocatalytic, the difference being that in autopoesis the process is self-originating rather than just self feeding. Both terms are important when thinking about change and the acceleration of change because they describe subtle but important attributes of systems undergoing change. (Maturana and Varela, *Autopoesis and Cognition*, 1974)

Behavioral Economics – Study of the effects of psychological, social, cognitive, and emotional factors on the economic decisions of individuals and institutions, and the consequences for market prices, returns, and resource allocation.

Bias – Factors that influence opinions and decisions are biases. There are many different types, six of the most notable are:
1. **Denial** (Anchoring Bias): Ignoring contradictory evidence.
2. **Just This Morning** (Availability Heuristic Bias): Vivid and easily imaginable events and recent events are weighted disproportionately in making decisions.
3. **Justification** (Confirmation Bias): Initial decisions become self-fulfilling prophesies, and data are collected after the event to justify the decision. Contradictory evidence is often disregarded.
4. **Escalation Bias**: Previous commitments tend to influence present decisions; this is often referred to as "putting good money after bad," and generally refers to our unwillingness to walk away after a bad investment.
5. **Framing Bias**: How a situation is presented affects the decision; and it can be easily even if unconsciously framed to validate a given expectation or position.
6. **Hindsight Bias**: It is easy to construct a logical narrative to explain events in hindsight, even when foresight had no clue what was coming.
(See Section 42: *Decision Shift*)

Biotechnology – Use of digital information about genetics to introduce changes into an individual's genome. Also referred to as 'mutagenesis,' or designed mutation. (See Section 24: *Gene Shift*; See also *CRISPR*)

Black Swan – Something that was thought to be impossible or nonexistent until it is subsequently discovered or occurs. More broadly, the cognitive fallacy of assuming that something cannot exist or could not occur just because it has not been seen or has not yet occurred. (Nassim Nicholas Taleb. *The Black Swan: The Impact of the Highly Improbable*. Random House, 2007. p. xvii.)

Blockchain – A software programming technique that embeds information in file that cannot be altered and is therefore suitable for storing financial records and related information that are not subject to coercion and corruption. The technical basis of Bitcoin. (See Section 21: *Blockchain Shift* and Section 77: *Blockchain Disruption*; See also *Cryptocurrency*)

Climate Refugees – People who become refugees as a result of climate change.

CEO Disease – The tendency to abandon the rigorous thinking efforts that led one to become CEO, once one has become the CEO.

Climageddon – A hypothetical and worst case outcome of climate change, the result that would occur from continued warming of the climate, the consequent melting of all the polar ice leading to significantly higher sea levels and thus major coastal flooding, while at the same time prolonged droughts, increased incidents of infectious diseases, and all the resulting human suffering and massive financial losses.

Co-Evolution – An evolutionary process in which two factors evolve as a consequence of their interaction. Used in title of an influential journal from the 1970s, *Co-Evolution Quarterly*.

Cognitive Dissonance – The tendency "to suppress, gloss over, water down or 'waffle' issues which would produce conflict or 'psychological pain' within an organization. (Barbara Tuchman, *The March of Folly*, p. 303) See also *Groupthink*.)

Cold Trade War – Conflict between China and the US over electronic hardware and software (Clay Shirky, *Little Rice*, p. 78)

Commuter Amnesia – Commuters tend to shut out their daily experiences of commuting to work, and to forget about commute trips as soon as they are done. (Charles Montgomery, *Happy City*, p. 180)

Complexity – In common language complexity is often confused with complicatedness, referring to something that can manifest in a lot of different ways. In more precise systems language complexity refers to the possible states of a system; more complex systems have more possible states. In most cases this is a consequence of having more inputs and/or more connections. Hence, complex systems such as the human brain (the most complex organ and possibly the

most complex biological system), are so deeply interconnected that its 80 billion neurons are connected by tens of *trillions* of synapses, resulting in an uncountable range of possible human behaviors.

Conspicuous non-consumption – A pattern of consumer consumption in which we show off our environmental awareness by letting others know how conscientious we can be, and how little we can consume. This is contrasted with "conspicuous consumption," the competitive act of consumption as a demonstration of wealth and power, common from the 1950s through the 1990s.

Counter-Intuitive – Something that behaves in ways that we do not expect, as it is contrary to our intuition. Typically refers to systems that do the opposite of what is expected and intended. These behaviors are generally due to the their very high complexity, which succeeds in fooling our intuition. (Jay Forrester, "Counter-Intuitive Behavior of Social Systems.")

CRISPR – A recently developed and advanced technique in biotechnology by which individual genes can be specifically targeted for modification, and which

transforms that practitioner into an 'evolution engineer.' (See also *Biotechnology*.)

Crony Capitalism – Quasi-capitalist national economy in which the friends and relations of a national leader enrich themselves through preferential treatment and corruption. The Economist reports that aggregate crony wealth is now a massive $1.75 trillion worldwide, although down from $2 trillion in 2014. (*The Economist*. "The Party Winds Down: Our crony-capitalism index." May 7, 2016.)

Cryptocurrency – An encrypted (hence 'crypto') digital currency that is technically based on the blockchain (see *Blockchain*) and which functions as an alternative to a state-sponsored government currency. Potentially revolutionary in that it could make government currencies obsolete. (See Section 21: *Blockchain Shift*)

Cultural Neuroscience – Study of the impact of human culture on human neurology, and particularly on the human brain. (Joseph Henrich, *The Secret of Our Success*, p. 268)

Cybersovereignty – The idea that the internet should have borders and controls for information to respect the sovereignty of nations.

(Clay Shirky, *Little Rice*, p. 27)

Davos Man – Member of the global elite who attends the annual World Economic Forum conference in Davos, Switzerland (Samuel Huntington)

D-Curve – The double curves implied by Moore's Law, the rising curve of exponential improvement in computer chip technology, and reciprocal downward curve of cost. Computers get rough twice as powerful and half as expensive, so 4x better, even 18 months or so. The curves drawn together form the shape of a D, hence the D-Curve.

Demand Destruction – Reduction in demand based on changing consumer patterns. For example, energy efficient appliances and light bulbs "destroy demand" for electricity, which in turn destroys demand for whatever is used to generate electricity, whether oil, coal, nuclear, or solar. (Peter Zeihan, *The Accidental Superpower*, p. 133: "If 3D printing captures just 1 percent of global manufacturing it will slice 50,000 bpd from global oil consumption just from transport savings.")

Digital Danger Zone – The period of history into which we are entering that is characterized by a profusion of new digital technologies of significant power that make it possible for new companies to threaten older ones.

Digital Economy – Hypothetically, the next economy following industrialism, into which we are now making the transition.

Disruption Map (D-Map) – The graph of a potentially disruptive technology or social trend. The intent is to anticipate future shifts in the market, or disruptions, in order to prepare strategically. By carefully gathering early warning signals, models can be assembled which may preview subsequent developments.

Economic Geography – The study of why some places grow and prosper compared to others. (Mario Polèse, *The Wealth & Poverty of Regions*, p. 1)

Elderpocalypse – The hypothetical result of the continuing aging of the population in conjunction with reduced birth rates. As the number of elderly people increases while the number of working adults decreases, the financial strains on national and local governments will become severe because of the costs of health care for the elderly will rise significantly while tax revenues will be shrinking.

Emergence – The appearance of unplanned and/or unexpected behaviors, often as a result of the conjunction of forces. Evolution and technology typically act on the form of a system, which enables new functions to then emerge. (See Section 44: *Emergence Shift*)

Energy Density – The amount of energy that can be extracted from a given mass or volume of a raw material. Oil has a very high energy density because one unit of oil can generally produce more useful work than the same unit mass or volume of nearly any other non-nuclear material. Due to oil's high energy density it is particularly challenging for non-fossil energy systems such as wind and solar to be economically competitive.

Ethnic Nationalism – Alignment of the historical or ethnic population of a region around a nationalist concept. (Clay Shirky, *Little Rice*, p 104)

Euro – The European Union common currency.
The word Euro has also become a popular prefix for an entire vocabulary of terms related to the EU:

Eurozone – The 19 EU members states that have adopted the Euro currency (9 have not).

Eurosceptic or Euroskeptic –

Someone who is feels that the EU is not a good idea.

Euroenthusiast – Someone who feels the opposite, that the EU is a good idea.

Eurosclerosis – Term coined by German economist Herbert Giersch in the 1970s, to describe a pattern of economic stagnation in Europe that may have resulted from government over-regulation and overly generous social benefits.

EuroStar – High speed train from London to Paris.

Evolutionary Happiness Function
A mathematical formula developed by economists Gary Becker and Luis Rayo which says that 'Happiness = your success minus your expectations, and is thus your perceived social status.' "The equation explains the psychological process that both fuels our desire for a bigger home, and ensures that we will be dissatisfied shortly after moving in. Humans do not perceive value in absolute terms. We compare what we have to what everyone else has, and then recalibrate the distance to the 'finish line of happiness.'" (Charles Montgomery, *Happy City*, p. 80)

Exit – Common suffix used in media denoting proposed, planned, or threatened departure of a member state from the European Union.

Brexit – Denotes the departure of Great Britain, voted by the British population in 2016. (Note also that should the British change their minds, as well they might, the process of rejoining the EU might be termed "Breconciliation.")

Grexit – Denotes the possible departure of Greece. Once this usage was widely accepted, usage of the term then spread. For example, this headline, "Can Germany engineer a coal exit" (*Science Magazine*, January 29, 2016) refers to the discontinuation of coal usage throughout Germany, a proposed national response to global climate change.

Texit – Hypothetical departure of Texas from the USA in the event of fragmentary forces lead to breakup of the nation. Of all states in the US, Texas maintains its separate identity perhaps most strongly and might be most likely to secede.

Exopolitics – Political relations between Earth and off-Earth sovereign entities, such as independent communities or "nations" inhabiting Earth orbit or other celestial bodies such as the moon or mars. It's science fiction today, but within a few decades it could become a reality. (Howell, Elizabeth. 'SpaceX's Elon Musk to Reveal Mars Colonization Ideas This Year.' *Space.com*. January 9, 2015.)

Financialization (of the economy) – The shift of progressively more economic activity to financial transactions rather than products or services.

Financialization (of citizenship) – The practice of buying citizenship in a country. (Atossa Araxia Abrahamian, *The Cosmopolites*, p. 84) See also *Investment-Based Citizenship*.

Floating Storage – With a glut of oil flooding the market leading supply to exceed demand, oil producers ran out of places to store it. Since there was also an abundance of oil tanker ships not needed for transporting oil, they were turned into storage facilities. Compare "rolling storage," which is the same concept applied to oil tanker railroad cars.

Freakonomics – A flashier name and book title pertaining to Behavioral Economics, the study of how behavior influences and is influenced by economics. Due to the success of the book the suffix "onomics" has become fashionable. (Steven D. Levitt and Stephen J. Dubner. *Freakonomics: A Rogue Economist Explores the Hidden Side of Everything*. William Morrow, 2009.) (See also

Narconomics.)

Frenemy – An entity that is simultaneously your friend and your adversary or enemy. China and the US, for example, have a massive volume of commercial trade between them, but also sustain difficult relations over a number of contentious topics.

Future Shock – Alvin Toffler coined this term in his book of the same title to describe how the acceleration of change creates adverse psychological reactions. (Toffler, Alvin. *Future Shock*. Random House, 1970.) (See also *Present Shock*)

Geometry of Conviviality – The study of the design of urban spaces to promote and enable convivial behavior. (Charles Montgomery, *Happy City*, p. 135) (See also, *Law of Social Geometry*.)

Geopolitics – The study of how place matters in the political dialog, and thus the political significance of geography for nations and cultures. (See *Geostrategy*.)

Geoprofiling – Software that analyzes times and geo coordinates of military actions along with related information about terrain, roads, ethnicity, tribal or civic alliances to identify the likely location of the attacking forces and/or locations of weapons caches. (*The Economist*. "Shrinking the haystack." January 16, 2016.)

Geostrategy – The strategy of a nation or region in relation to other nations, studied from the perspective of geographical factors and features such as oceans, mountains, etc. For example, Russia has no substantial geographical features separating it from its European neighbors to the west, and is therefore vulnerable to land attack. The US, in contrast, is protected by massive oceans on both east and west, which provide natural barriers to potential aggressors. (See *Geopolitics*.)

Gerontocracy – Societies with a significant or growing proportions of elderly citizens. These societies will significantly increase in number in the coming decades. (Peter Zeihan, *The Accidental Superpower*, p. 149)

Globalization – Progressive engagement of all nations in one global economic system.

Great Firewall of China, GFW – (Officially, the Golden Shield) The name of the data filters used to prevent information from coming into China from the outside world via the internet. A combination of automation and human oversight.

Groupthink – The tendency of executive teams and decision making bodies to align on a shared view of an uncertain trend or future event based not on the data about that event, but on a shared but generally unspoken desire to maintain a convivial and collegial atmosphere. Dissent is discouraged, which leads to deficiencies in decisions adopted. Identified by Irving Janis in his book of the same name.

Hedonic Utility – Emotional benefits of a given activity.

Hedonic Treadmill – The tendency of humans to increase our expectations as our fortunes improve, leaving us perpetually dissatisfied. (Charles Montgomery, *Happy City*, p. 11)

HENRY, High Earner Not Rich Yet – A young person, usually highly educated, who has a high paying job but has not yet accumulated significant wealth. Considered a good credit risk by the start-up financial services firm SoFi, which has pioneered personal loans and mortgages to HENRYs. SoFi received an investment of $1 billion from SoftBank ventures in September 2015. (*The Economist*. "So far, so good." January 16, 2016.)

Honor Culture – (Or culture of honor) – Cultural norms based around the concept of honor and the need for particularly men to protect and defend it, often through intimidation and violence. (Nisbitt and Cohen, "Insult, Aggression, and the Southern Culture of Honor." *Journal of Personality and Social Psychology*, Vol 70, No 5, 1996)

Hyper-connectedness – When everything is connected to everything, then anything can happen. (See *Omni-connectedness*)

IED, Improvised Explosive Device – A bomb made from a cell phone or similar device and some explosive, and able to be detonated remotely via a phone call. A particularly destructive weapon in an urban civil war setting. Developed in Iraq and Afghanistan by forces opposing the American occupations there, and which caused hundreds of American casualties.

Improvisational Intelligence – The human capacity provided by evolution to improvise to attain objectives based on a general understanding of how the world works. (Joseph Henrich, *The Secret of Our Success*, p. 11)

Indefensible Space – Featureless space between buildings that collects garbage and attracts crime. (Charles Montgomery *Happy City*, p. 131)

Internally-Displaced Person – A citizen of a given nation who has been forced from their home due to civil war, natural disaster, or another traumatic event, but remains within the same nation. (Compare: *Refugee*)

Investment-Based Citizenship – The practice of buying citizenship in a country. (Atossa Araxia Abrahamian, *The Cosmopolites*, p 84) (See *Financialization of Citizenship*).

J-Curve – Any process that, when graphed, is revealed to grow exponentially, and thus mimics the shape of the letter "J". (See *Moore's Law*.)

Jevons's Paradox – Any situation in which efficiency improvements lead to more, not less, consumption. "More fuel-efficient steam engines didn't lead to less coal consumption. Better engines made energy use effectively less expensive, and helped move the world to an industrial ear powered by coal." (Edward Glaeser, *Triumph of the City*, p. 37) Henry Ford also understood this.

Killer Robot – Robots designed for criminal or military purposes. (Also known as a *killbot*.)

Law of Accelerating Returns – In some social and market settings, those who have more get still more. These markets do not tend to balance out, but rather to concentrate more and more resources under the ownership of fewer and fewer people.

Law of Social Geometry – Behavior by people, particularly in their front yards, that defines the ideal separation between the public street or sidewalk and the individual residence, enabling sociability and privacy at the same time. Identified by Jan Gehl at 10.6 feet. (See also *Geometry of Conviviality*.)

Lead User Innovation – When the most intensive user of a product understands its utility best, and their adaptations and modifications are often adopted into the standard product.

Leading Indicator – A signal from the external environment suggesting an impending change. Often identified as part of the scenario planning process. Very useful for planning and strategy, as receipt of leading indicators supports proactive rather than reactive planning and management. (See also, *Scenario Planning; Weak Signal; Weak Signal Research*)

Learning
Joseph Henrich identifies 3 types:

Cultural Learning – Subclass of Social Learning based on specific factors of human-specific culture, such as inferences about the preferences, goals, prestige, and strategies adopted or exhibited by others, and by copying the actions of others.

Individual Learning – Learning through direct observation of and interaction with the environment. Note that the process of learning is identical to and yet the inverse of the process of creating. Hence, learning occurs when one's creativity is directed inwardly (creating the self), while creativity is when one's learning is directed outwardly (learning about the environment).

Social Learning – How an individual's learning is influenced by others.

(Henrich, Joseph. *The Secret of Our Success*, pp 12-13)

Milgram's Theory of Overload – How people respond to situations of excessive density of people and cars. "You cope by either ignoring the people around you or doing subtle battle with them." (Charles Montgomery, *Happy City*, p. 225)

Mind Uploading – Copying the contents of a person's brain into a computer. A theoretical possibility only, until the advent of superintelligent AI.

Moore's Law – Named for Intel Corporation co-founder Gordon Moore, describes exponential improvement in the performance of computer chip technology. Moore identified this phenomenon in 1965 and published an article about it, which resulted in the name Moore's Law being applied to it. (See *J-Curve*.)

Mutual Insecurity – Interactions between two nations characterized by insecurity on both sides as a consequence of not being able to anticipate or understand the actions and intents of the other. (Henry Kissinger, *World Order*, p. 336)

Narconomics – The economics (really finances) of illegal narcotics businesses, which are converging on the same set of management principles as are generally used by multinational corporations, namely hierarchical structures, human resources policies, metrics and rewards, etc. (Tom Wainwright, *Narconomics: How to Run a Drug Cartel*.) (See also *Freakonomics*)

Nature Deprivation – Lack of natural beauty in a given location or accessible to a given person. "Buildings that look out on trees and grass experience about half of the violent crime of buildings that look out on barren courtyards." (Charles Montgomery, *Happy City*, p. 110)

NEET, Not in Employment, Education, or Training – Typically a young person whose future prospects are not so bright. (*The Economist*, January 23, 2016)

Neoliberalism – An economic ideology which holds that the economic system should be structured to favor capital over other elements of production. Primary driving force behind *Globalization* and *Financialization* of the economy. Not appreciated by much of the world because of the unwanted side effects it causes.

Neuromorphic – Computer hardware designed to as closely as possible resemble the neural architecture of the brain. (Murray Shanahan, *The Technological Singularity*, p. 32)

Non-Genetic Evolutionary Process – Evolutionary processes that are cultural rather than genetic, such as new capabilities and behaviors that emerge not based on genetic mutation, but because of learning. With the acceleration of change, non-genetic processes are having increasingly significant effects on the overall evolutionary process. (Joseph Henrich, *The Secret of Our Success*, p. 35)

Non-Place – A place where people do not want to be. (Charles Montgomery, *Happy City*, p. 168)

Non-State Actor – An entity of geopolitical significance that is not a nation-state. This is therefore typically a church or religion, a corporation, particularly a large, multi-national one, or a large-scale criminal enterprise that works across national boundaries. (See also "TCO," or *Transnational Criminal Organization*)

Obseogenic – Literally, fat-making. Social and cultural factors that promote obesity in humans, such as diet choices, lack of exercise, and urban designs that discourage exercise. (Charles Montgomery, *Happy City*, p. 95)

Observer Effect – Once we begin to measure something, such as an economic variable, its behavior starts to change. "If the government starts to artificially take steps to inflate housing prices, they might well increase, but they will no longer be good

measures of economic health." (Nate Silver, *The Signal and the Noise*, p. 188)

ODMS, On-Demand Mobile Services – The tendency of service providers to offer a complete service experience via apps that aggregate consumer demand on mobile devices, but fulfill that demand through offline services. (Source: Steve Schlafman: http://schlaf.me/post/81679927670) (See also *Uberification*.)

Omni-connectedness – Everything is connected to everything. (See also *Hyper-connectedness*)

Overshoot – Excessive consumption of natural resources; refers to "overshooting" the productive capacity of Earth, i.e., using more than is produced. Technically it is possible to overshoot over a given period of time due to accumulated stocks, but overshoot cannot be sustained indefinitely. For example, underground water tables that store water over a period of years or decades can provide water for agriculture, but if the water is drawn out faster than it is replenished then it will one day run out entirely.

Phase 3 – Refers to the three phases of human history. Phase 1 is the Agricultural Era; Phase 2 is the Industrial Era; and Phase 3 is the

Digital Era we are now entering. The defining point of entry is the graph of human population, which by its very shape suggests that Phase 2 is now ending as the rate of population growth that characterized Phase 2 is slowing. Demographers expect that slowing to continue based on historical rates of urbanization and reproductive rates in urban families. As more than 50 percent of the population is urbanized and urbanized families tend to have 2 or fewer children, the population explosion of 1800 – 2000 is coming to an end of its own accord.

Population Implosion – Declining population of a region, nation, or globally due to declining birthrate, in some cases combined with accelerated mortality. Japan and most nations of Eastern Europe are currently experiencing population implosions, that is, their overall populations are in decline. As humanity continues to urbanize, it is likely that the overall birth rate will peak in the 2040 – 2050 time frame, and decline thereafter, again, based on current trends. Population implosion will have decisive and potentially adverse consequences economically, as modern capitalism has never dealt with this situation, and is structured to benefit from population growth.

Post-Biological – Living systems and processes that are no longer only biological, but which include in part or in total those that are technological and/or digitally enabled.

Post-Human – Along the evolutionary line a being that is no longer human but whose ancestors were human. The existence of post-humans is speculated but has not yet been demonstrated / achieved. In particular, it is expected that long-duration space flight and off-Earth habitation over multiple generations will result in the development of post-humans because they will be living and thus evolving under fundamentally different conditions than those residing on Earth. While this was once a matter of science fiction it is now a matter of legal speculation and if the Space Age continues it will be a matter of law within a century or two. (See also *Trans-Human*)

Power Density – The amount of power (work) capable of being produced by a given resource. Similar to "energy density" but referring specifically to the work accomplished rather than the potential of work to be accomplished.

Power Vacuum – In politics and geopolitics, when established authorities in a nation or society are removed by force, or they collapse due to internal causes, the resulting void often devolves into chaos. Riots and looting are local examples, as when police or army cannot contain a mob and they run wild. On a national scale, and particularly when an authoritarian government is removed, the resulting power vacuum often leads to chaos. In the majority of cases new authority figures step forward and seize control. In recent history, the removal of Saddam Hussein from power in Iraq was not accompanied by a major input of authority, and the result was national chaos. Eventually ISIS emerged as a brutal authority figure in some parts of the country, capitalizing upon the vacuum to seize power.

Practical Isolation – As in, "the strategy of practical isolation," that is, the strategy adopted by the Chinese government to keep its citizens isolated from news and events of the world outside of China to prevent the seeds of domestic unrest. (Clay Shirky, *Little Rice*, p. 122)

Precision Agriculture – Application of digital technology to improve the efficiency of farming and to increase yields. Sensor arrays installed in farm fields measure soil moisture and chemical composition, enabling farmers to apply water and chemicals much more efficiently. Farms are thus becoming small-scale digital factories, with many sensors feeding data via wireless networks to the farmhouse and then to the tractors. Drones are also being used extensively to monitor crops and to deliver chemicals as well. Also known as 'agri-tech.'

Precision Medicine – Therapies and treatments customized for individual patients, often using a combination of genetic sequencing of the patient and/or of the malady, as in the case of cancer. (See also, *Genetic Medicine*)

Present Shock – Douglas Rushkoff coined this play on words, building upon Alvin Toffler's concept of Future Shock, to describe the psychological impact that occurs when too much is happening simultaneously. (Rushkoff, Douglas. *Present Shock: When Everything Happens Now*. Current, 1994.) (See also *Future Shock*)

Refugee – A person who flees their home or native country due to persecution, civil war, natural disaster, etc. (See also *Internally-*

Displaced Person)

Reverse Mentoring – Mentoring is a normal cultural process wherein people with more experience and expertise share advice with less. Typically this occurs when older people help or support younger ones. In reverse mentoring, however, the point is that the acceleration of change has made the knowledge of the older ones obsolete, while the younger ones have often more quickly and readily adopted new ideas and technologies, and so they coach the older ones on how to utilize all the new stuff, and what it might mean for their organizations and institutions.

Scenario Planning – A planning or thinking approach in which we determine the likely driving forces in a given situation, and then model various possible states of those forces through thought experiments, with the intent of modeling the future without making specific predictions. (See Section 63: *Scenario Planning Shift*)

Seastead – Hypothetical human-made islands in international waters outside of the jurisdiction of any nation, a project undertaken by entrepreneur Peter Thiel.

Self-domestication – As a result of the impact of human culture, evolution has favored the development of certain qualities in humans that include being inclined to social behavior, following established norms and rules, monitoring behavior of others, and sanctioning those who do not follow them. (Joseph Henrich, *The Secret of Our Success*, p. 5)

Selective Attention – The principle that people pay attention to a limited range of inputs, and select what to pay attention to according to personal and cultural biases.

Shadowtime – How it feels to live simultaneously in an uncertain present and a future with the potential to be dramatically different. Source: "The Bureau of Linguistical Reality."
"The Bureau of Linguistical Reality is a public participatory artwork by Heidi Quante and Alicia Escott focused on creating new language as an innovative way to better understand our rapidly changing world due to manmade climate change and other Anthropocenic events." https://bureauoflinguisticalreality.com/

Singularity – The anticipated point in time at which computers become so capable they have human or human-like cognition and are able to create copies of themselves and/or additional computers that can learn from one another, such that the learning process proceeds exponentially, at which point the vector of human and computer evolution speeds up in a way that is at present incomprehensible. Or more simply, the point at which everything changes because computers become smarter than people. Also referred to as the "technological singularity." (Ray Kurzweil, *The Singularity is Near*, Random House, 2005.)

Social Deficit – Lack of opportunity to socialize with other people. "We can meet almost all of our needs without gathering in public." (Charles Montgomery, *Happy City*, p. 153)

Soft Power – The influence of culture on a society, as distinct from hard power, the influence of force. (Joseph Nye, *The Paradox of American Power*, Oxford, 2003.)

Stalker Economy – Massive databases compiled on individuals based on their online purchases. (Al Gore, *The Future*, p. 370)

Suicide-by-Cop – Someone who commits suicide by starting a gun battle with the police in the expectation and hope of being killed.

Surveillance State – Use of advanced technology by the state to keep track of everyone and everything.

Swanson Effect – The declining cost of solar panels as a result of technical improvements through research and development. Named after Richard Swanson, the founder of SunPower Corporation.

Systems Thinking – The process of trying to understand, or understanding, the behavior of a system, and presumably a complex one, through disciplined study.

Television Effect – Impact of the introduction of television into a community. "When TV service was introduced to otherwise healthy communities in Canada in the 1980s, it has an almost immediate corrosive effect on civic participation. Watching TV correlates with higher material aspirations, more anxiety, lower financial satisfaction, lower trust in other, and less frequent social activity." (Charles Montgomery, *Happy City*, p. 154)

Thinking Types – There are different thinking approaches to challenges and intellectual problems including forecasting and decision making under uncertainty.

Counterfactual Thinking – Thinking about how something may have turned out differently than it did, useful when assessing the chain of events that resulted in a given outcome, and considering how slight changes along the chain may have resulted in quite different outcomes.

Probabilistic Thinking – Thinking based on a clear grasp of the nature of probabilities. A probabilistic thinker recognizes that if a future event is forecast to occur with 70% probability, this also means that there's a 30% likelihood that it will not occur. This is notable because of the common error that anything over 50% probability is taken as a prediction that it will occur. "A probabilistic thinker will be less distracted by 'why' questions and focus on 'how.' This is no semantic quibble. 'Why?' directs us to metaphysics; 'How?' sticks with physics." Philip Tetlock. *Superforecasting*, Crown, 2015. p. 150.

Trained Incapacity – As trained capacity is learned skill, trained incapacity is learned non-skill, i.e., having learned how *not* to do something.

Trans-Human – The developed of evolutionarily advanced species that evolves beyond humans because of advanced capabilities, either cognitive and computational or physical. Simply, super-people. (See also *Post-Human*)

Transnational Criminal Organization (TCO) – A large criminal enterprise that works across national boundaries. Typically involved in drugs, money laundering, human smuggling, and prostitution.

Uberification – The tendency of companies to emulate the Uber business model, which combines multiple elements and is therefore somewhat complex to execute, but when done well it is a high-value-added approach. It includes a smart phone app that provides mobile access, a built-in payment mechanism, and delivery of a service. Generally highly disruptive to established business models. (See also *ODMS, On-Demand Mobile Services*)

UHNWI, Ultra-high net worth individual – A very rich person. (Atossa Araxia Abrahamian, *The Cosmopolites*, p. 72)

Undercrowding – Insufficient urban density to create successful and self-sustaining urban environments. Typical of cities such as Detroit that are radically contracting due to changes in industry or the economy. Also typical of wealthy suburban neighborhoods whose residents must consume disproportionately a high volume of resources to sustain their lifestyles. (William Whyte, Project for Public Spaces)

Unicorn – A mythical creature, or a start-up technology company that achieves a high valuation of more than $1 billion among investors, although it has not yet sold any stock publicly. Recent examples include Alibaba and Uber.

Urban Ponzi Scheme – New real estate development in suburbs creates short term benefits in the form of development fees, tax revenues, and construction jobs, but create long term costs that pileup faster than cities can pay them, in the form of infrastructure maintenance, health care costs, and subsidies for public transit systems that are not self-sustaining. On a wider social basis, suburban dwellers consume more natural resources and create more pollution per person than urban residents. (Charles Montgomery, *Happy City*, p. 260) (See also *Undercrowding*, of which sprawling suburbs are an example.)

Urban Poverty Paradox – "Any attempt to fix the poverty level in a single city may well backfire and increase the level of poverty in a city by attracting more poor people." (Edward Glaeser, *Triumph of the City*, p. 76). The same thing applies to Syrian refugees.

Vancouverism – Designs of cities that copy the elements of Vancouver, Canada, which is considered to be one of the world's best designed cities. (Charles Montgomery, *Happy City*, p. 118)

Weak Signal; Weak Signal Research – Research focusing on identifying early indications of change. Particular useful in the context of scenario planning efforts, by identifying weak signals that we may be able to carefully discern in the environment, we get early warning of impending change, and can then act in anticipation, pro-act, rather than afterwards, re-act. (See also, Leading Indicator; Scenario Planning)

ACKNOWLEDGMENTS

The way of looking at the world I describe here was helped into being largely because of rich and inspiring interactions I've had during the past few years with high school students (at Granada High School, Livermore, California) and college students (primarily at FIT, Fashion Institute of Technology, New York City, and also in China, Kenya, Malaysia, New Zealand, and Pakistan, where recent travels have taken me).

My goal was to convey to them the awareness that the world for which their institutions have been diligently preparing them has already faded away. Further, the expectations for the future and the world views implicitly and often explicitly espoused by those institutions is already obsolete, the remnants of a lost world.

I wanted to help the students to understand that a new world is arriving quickly, and I wanted them to grasp what it might be like, and in so doing to help them begin to recognize how they can contribute to making it better.

This book has some brothers and sisters, prior books on related topics, including especially *Foresight and Extreme Creativity: Strategy for the 21st Century*, which I wrote to summarize learnings from a decade of fascinating consulting assignments we have completed around the world. *The Big Shift* builds further upon that foundation, and I am deeply grateful to everyone I've interacted with on the way to completing this story. I hope they, and you, have found it worthwhile and enlightening.

ABOUT THE AUTHOR

Langdon Morris is one of the world's top thinkers and authors on innovation and strategy. He is co-founder and Senior Partner of InnovationLabs, one of the world's leading innovation consultancies, President of FutureLab, a global strategy and technology incubator, and innovation council co-lead at Red Team Engineering.

His work focuses on developing and applying advanced methods in innovation and strategy to solve complex problems with very high levels of creativity. His original and ground-breaking ideas have been adopted worldwide.

Among his recent clients are firms, governments, and non-profit organizations including Airbus, Aspen Institute, American Board of Medical Specialties, Callaghan New Zealand, Covance, France Telecom/Orange, Gemalto, Kaiser Permanente, Total Oil, UNICEF, the U.S. Coast Guard, the U.S. Department of Defense, and many others.

He is a frequent and much-appreciated keynote speaker at conferences and corporate events, and is author or co-author twelve books, including some of the most important titles in the field of innovation of the last decade, and editor of the five books in the Aerospace Technology Working Group series on the future of space travel and space commerce.

He is formerly Innovation Coordinator at Fashion Institute of Technology (FIT, New York), and Senior Practice Scholar at the Ackoff Center of the University of Pennsylvania. He has taught MBA courses in innovation and strategy at the Ecole Nationale des Ponts et Chaussées (France) and Universidad de Belgrano (Argentina), and has lectured at universities on 4 continents, including Chaoyang University of Technology (Taiwan), Conservatoire Nationale des Arts et Métiers (France), Rochester Institute of Technology (USA), Shanghai Jao Tong University (China), and the University of Nairobi.

ALSO BY LANGDON MORRIS

Blockchain Manifesto
with Moses Ma and Po Chi Wu

Foresight and Extreme Creativity
Strategy for the 21st Century

Agile Innovation
with Moses Ma and Po Chi Wu

Soulful Branding
with Jerome Conlon and Moses Ma

The Innovation Formula

The Chief Innovation Officer

The Agile Innovation Master Plan

Permanent Innovation

4th Generation R&D
with William L. Miller

The Knowledge Channel

Managing the Evolving Corporation

ATWG Aerospace Books
Series Editor

Space for the 21st Century

International Cooperation for the Development of Space

Space Commerce

Living in Space

Beyond Earth

REFERENCES

PART 1: WORLD SHIFT

1 STRUCTURE, NEXT ECONOMY, INDUSTRIAL ECONOMICS

Atkinson, Anthony. *Inequality: What Can Be Done?* Harvard University Press, 2015.

Bruecker, Jan K. *Lectures on Urban Economics.* MIT Press, 2011.

Chandler, Alfred D. Jr. *Scale and Scope: The Dynamics of Industrial Capitalism.* Harvard/Belknap, 1990.

De Soto, Hernando. *The Mystery of Capital: Why Capitalism Triumphs in the West and Fails Everywhere Else.* Basic Books, 2000.

Donovan, Paul. *The Truth About Inflation.* Routledge, 2015.

Dovey, Kim. *Framing Places: Mediating Power in Built Form.* Routledge, 1999.

Fuller, Buckminster. *Anthology for a New Millennium.* Thomas T. K. Zung, Editor. St. Martin's Press, 2001.

Gordon, Robert J. *The Rise and Fall of American Growth.* Princeton University Press, 2016.

King, Stephen D. *Grave New World: The End of Globalization and the Return of History.* Yale University Press, 2017.

Krugman, Paul. *The Return of Depression Economics.* Norton, 2000.

Lechner, Frank J. and John Boli. *The Globalization Reader.* Wiley, 2015.

Mason, Paul. *Postcapitalism: A Guide to Our Future.* Farrar, Strauss and Giroux, 2015.

Mayer-Schonberger and Thomas Ramge. *Reinventing Capitalism in the Age of Big Data.* Basic Books, 2018.

Mead, Walter Russell. "The Big Shift: How Democracy Fails Its Way to Success." *Foreign Affairs,* May/June 2018.

Milanovic, Branko. *Global Inequality: A New Approach for the Age of Globalization.* The Belknap Press of Harvard University, 2016.

Piketty, Thomas. *Capital in the Twenty-First Century.* The Belknap Press of Harvard University, 2017.

Polèse, Mario. *The Wealth and Poverty of Regions: Why Cities Matter.* The University of Chicago Press, 2009.

Perkins, John. *The New Confessions of an Economic Hit Man.* Berrett-Kohler Publishers, Inc., 2016.

Schumpeter, Joseph. *Can Capitalism Survive? Creative Destruction and the Future of the Global Economy.* Harper Perennial, 1942, 1976.

Schumpeter, Joseph. *Capitalism, Socialism, and Democracy.* Harper & Brothers, 1942.

Sharma, Ruchir. *The Rise and Fall of Nations: Forces of Change in the Post-Crisis World.* WW Norton, 2016.

Short, John Rennie and Yeong-Hyun Kim. *Globalization and the City.* Addison Wesley Longman Limited, 1999.

Short, John Rennie. *Urban Theory: A Critical Assessment.* Palgarve, 2006

Spence, Michael. *The Next Convergence: The Future of Economic Growth in a Multispeed World.* 2011.

Thurow, Lester C. *The Future of Capitalism: How Today's Economic Forces Shape Tomorrow's World.* Morrow, 1996.

Watson, Peter. *Ideas: A History of Thought and Invention, from Fire to Freud.* HarperPerrennial, 2006.

Zingales, Luigi. *A Capitalism for the People: Recapturing the Lost Genius of American Prosperity.* Basic Books, 2012.

4 LAND SHIFT: FARM, CLIMATE, ENERGY

Brown, Lester R. *Plan B 2.0: Rescuing a Planet Under Stress and a Civilization in Trouble.* Norton, 2006.

Dawson, Ashley. *Extreme Cities: The Peril and Promise of Urban Life in the Age of Climate Change.* Verso, 2017.

Martenson, Chris, PhD. *The Crash Course: The Unsustainable Future of Our Economy, Energy, and Environment.* Wiley, 2011.

Lewis, Joanna I. *Green Innovation in China: China's Wind Power Industry and the Global Transition to a Low-Carbon Economy.* Columbia University Press, 2013.

Prentiss, Mara. *Energy Revolution: The Physics and the Promise of Efficient Technology.* Belknap Harvard, 2015.

Engdahl, F. William. *A Century of War: Anglo-American Oil Politics and the New World Order.* Progressive Press, 2012.

Heintzman, Andrew and Evan Solomon, Editors. *Fueling the Future: How the Battle Over Energy is Changing Everything.* Anansi, 2003.

Jaffe, Amy Myers. "Green Giant: Renewable Energy and Chinese Power." *Foreign Affairs,* March/April 2018.

Smil, Vaclav. *Global Catastrophes and Trends: The Next Fifty Years.* MIT Press, 2008.

Smil, Vaclav. *Oil.* Oneworld, 2008.

Yeang, Ken, Shireen Jahnkassim, Humadedah Rosly and Robert Powell. *Constructed Ecosystems: Ideas and Subsystems in the Work of Ken Yeang.* Applied Research + Design Publishing, 2016

Yergin, Daniel and Joseph Stanislaw. *The Commanding Heights: The Battle for the World Economy.* Free Press, 2002

Yergin, Daniel. *The Prize: The Epic Quest for Oil, Money & Power.* Free Press, 2008

8 LABOR SHIFT: COMPUTER CHIP, DIGITAL, ROBOT, SINGULARITY, URBAN, DEMOGRAPHIC, POPULATION, EUROPEAN

Arthur, W. Brian. *The Nature of Technology: What It Is and How It Evolves.* Free Press, 2009.

Batty, Michael. *The New Science of Cities.* MIT Press, 2017.

Brand, Stewart. *The Media Lab: Inventing the Future at M.I.T.* Penguin, 1987.

Brugmann, Jeb. *Welcome to the Urban Revolution: How Cities Are Changing the World.* Bloomsbury Press, 2009.

Clark, Greg. *Global Cities: A Short History.* Brookings, 2016.

Clark, David. *Urban World/Global City.* Routledge, 1996.

Diamandis, Peter H. and Steven Kotler. *Abundance: The Future Is Better Than You Think.* Free Press, 2102.

Dovey, Kim. *Urban Design Thinking: A Conceptual Toolkit.* Bloomsbury, 2016.

Ehrlich, Paul R. *The Population Bomb.* Ballantine Books, 1968.

Ellul, Jacques. *The Technological Society.* Knopf, 1964.

Glaeser, Edward. *Triumph of the City: How Our Greatest Invention Makes Us Richer, Smarter, Greener, Healthier, and Happier.* Penguin Books, 2011.

Hall, Peter. *Cities in Civilization.* Fromm International, 1998.

Hall, Peter. *Cities of Tomorrow: An Intellectual History of Urban Planning and Design Since 1880.* Wiley, 2014.

Jacobs, Jane. *Cities and the Wealth of Nations: Principles of Economic Life.* Random House, 1984.

Klimburg, Alexander. *The Darkening Web: The War for Cyberspace.* Penguin, 2018.

Kodama, Fumio. *Emerging Patterns of Innovation: Sources of Japan's Technological Edge.* Harvard Business School Press, 1991.

Kurzweil, Ray. *The Singularity is Near.* Penguin Books, 2005.

Litan, Robert E. *Trillion Dollar Economists: How Economists and Their Ideas Have Transformed Business.* Wiley/Bloomberg, 2014.

Marshall, Richard. *Emerging Urbanity: Global Urban Projects in the Asia Pacific Rim.* Spon Press, 2003.

Montgomery, Charles. *Happy City: Transforming Our Lives Through Urban Design.* Farrar, Strauss and Giroux. 2013. P. 181.

Moravec, Hans. *Mind Children: The Future of Robot and Human Intelligence.* Harvard University Press, 1988.

Piel, Gerard. *The Acceleration of History.* Knopf, 1972.

Shanahan, Murray. *The Technological Singularity.* MIT Press, 2015.

Venter, J. Craig. *Life at the Speed of Light: From the Double Helix to the Dawn of Digital Life.* Viking, 2013.

Yoos, Jennifer and Vincent James. *Parallel Cities: The Multilevel Metropolis.* Walker Art Center, 2016.

17 CAPITAL SHIFT: COMMODITIZATION, DEBT, FINANCIALIZATION, BLOCKCHAIN, TECHNOLOGY, HEALTH CARE, GENE, WARFARE

Braudel, Fernand. *The Structures of Everyday Life: Civilization and Capitalism, 15th-18th Century.* (3 Volumes) Harper & Row, 1982.

"The Gene-Editing Revolution." *Foreign Affairs,* May/June 2018.

Ma, Moses, Po Chi Wu and Langdon Morris. *The Blockchain Revolution.* FutureLab Press, 2018.

McMahon, Dinny. *China's Great Wall of Debt.* Houghton Mifflin Harcourt, 2018.

Mukherjee, Siddhartha. *The Gene: An Intimate History.* Scribner, 2016.

Scharre, Paul. *Army of None: Autonomous Weapons and the Future of War.* Norton, 2018.

Smith, Rupert. *The Utility of Force: The Art of War in the Modern World.* Knopf, 2005, 2007

"The Future of War." *The Economist* Special Report. January 27, 2018.

Surowiecki, James. *The Wisdom of Crowds: Why the Many Are Smarter Than the Few.* Abacus, 2004.

Venter, J. Craig. *Life at the Speed of Light: From the Double Helix to the Dawn of Digital Life.* Viking, 2013.

26 ENTREPRENEUR SHIFT: FUNDING, OUTER SPACE, GEOPOLITICS

Bhidé, Amar V. *The Origin and Evolution of New Businesses.* Oxford University Press, 2000.

Bremmer, Ian. *Superpower: Three Choices for America's Role in the World.* Penguin Portfolio, 2015.

Gyorffy, Laszlo and Lisa Friedman. *Creating Value with CO-STAR: An Innovation Tool for Perfecting and Pitching Your Brilliant Idea.* Enterprise Development Group, Inc., 2012.

Keegan, John. *Intelligence in War: Knowledge of the Enemy from Napoleon to Al-Qaeda.* Alfred A. Knopf, 2003.

Kissinger, Henry. *World Order.* Penguin, 2014.

Morris, Langdon and Kenneth J. Cox, Editors. *International Cooperation for the Development of Space.* ATWG Books, 2012.

Morris, Langdon and Kenneth J. Cox, Editors. *Space Commerce: The Inside Story by the People Who Are Making It Happen.* ATWG Books, 2010.

Ries, Eric. *The Lean Startup: How Today's Entrepreneurs Use Continuous Innovation to Create Radically Successful Businesses.* Crown Business, 2011.

Simpson, Michael, Ray Williamson and Langdon Morris. *Space for the 21st Century: Discovery, Innovation, Sustainability.* ATWG Books, 2016.

Sutherland, Benjamin, Editor. *Modern Warfare, Intelligence and Deterrence: The Technologies that Are Changing Them.* Wiley, 2011.

Zakaria, Fareed. *The Post-American World.* Norton, 2008, 2009.

Zeihan, Peter. *The Accidental Superpower: The Next Generation of American Preeminence and The Coming Global Disorder.* Twelve, 2014.

PART 2: MINDSET SHIFT

33 NEXT ECONOMY SHIFT: DIGITALIZATION, CREATIVE, METAPHOR, EXPECTATION, MEASUREMENT

Araya, Daniel and Michael A. Peters, Editors. *Education in the Creative Economy.* Peter Lang, 2010.

Carey, Benedict. *The Surprising Truth About How We Learn and Why It Happens.* Random House, 2014.

Florida, Richard. *The Rise of the Creative Class, Revisited.* Basic Books, 2011, 2012.

Friedman, Thomas L. *The World is Flat: A Brief History of the Twenty-First Century.* Farrar, Strauss and Giroux, 2005, 2006

Gill, Amy, Editor. *The Future of Public Space.* Metropolis Books, 2017.

Hartley, John, Wen Wen, and Henry Siling Li. *Creative Economy and Culture: Challenges, Changes and Futures for the Creative Industries.* Sage Publications, 2015.

Harvey, David. *A Brief History of Neoliberalism.* Oxford, 2005.

Harvey, David. *Marx, Capital and the Madness of Economic Reason.* Oxford, 2018.

Landsburg, Steven E. *The Armchair Economist: Economics & Everyday Life.* The Free Press, 1993.

Philipson, Dirk. *The Little Big Number: How GDP Came to Rule the World and What to Do About It.* Princeton University Press, 2015.

Polyani, Karl. *The Great Transformation: The Political and Economic Origins of Our Time.* Beacon Press, 2001.

Ross, Alec. *The Industries of the Future.* Simon & Schuster, 2016.

Sassen, Saskia. *Cities in a World Economy.* Sage, 2012.

Varoufakis, Yanis. *Adults in the Room.* Farrar, Straus, and Giroux, 2017.

Wolf, Martin. *Fixing Global Finance.* The Johns Hopkins University Press, 2008, 2010.

39 NEW PATTERN SHIFT: PARADIGM, STAIRCASE, DECISION, SCIENCE, EMERGENCE

Ariely, Dan. *Predictably Irrational: The Hidden Forces that Shape Our Decisions.* Harper, 2008.

Barber, Benjamin R. *Jihad vs. McWorld: Terrorism's Challenge to Democracy.* Ballantine Books, 1995.

Chabris, Christopher and Daniel Simons. *The Invisible Gorilla and Other Ways Our Institutions Deceive Us.* Crown Books, 2010.

Fuller, Buckminster, *Operating Manual for Spaceship Earth.* Clarion, 1970.

Fuller, R. Buckminster, Arthur L. Loeb (Introduction), E. J. Applewhite (Collaborator). *Synergetics: Explorations in the Geometry of Thinking.* MacMillan, 1982

Hellebrtandt, Tomas and Paolo Mauro. *World on the Move: Consumption Patterns in a More Equal Global Economy.* Peterson Institute for International Economics, 2016.

Holland, John. *Emergence: From Chaos to Order.* Persues Books, 1998.

Jantsch, Erich. *The Self-Organizing Universe.* Pergamon, 1980.

Johnson, Steven. *Emergence: The Connected Lives of Ants, Brains, Cities, and Software.* Touchstone, 2001.

Kahneman, Daniel. *Thinking, Fast and Slow.* Farrar, Straus and Giroux, 2011.

Kuhn, Thomas S. *The Essential Tension: Selected Studies in Scientific Tradition and Change.* Chicago, 1977.

Kuhn, Thomas S. *The Structure of Scientific Revolutions.* The University of Chicago Press, 1962, 1970.

Mansfield, Guy. *Developing Your Leadership Skills: From the Changing World to Changing the World.* 2013.

Mlodinow, Leonard. *Subliminal: How Your Subconscious Mind Rules Your Behavior.* Vintage, 2012.

Naisbett, John. *Megatrends: Then New Directions Transforming Our Lives.* Warner Books, 1982.

Ohmae, Kenichi. *The End of the Nation State: The Rise of Regional Economies.* Free Press, 1995.

Russo, J. Edward and Paul J.H. Schoemaker. *Winning Decisions: Getting It Right the First Time.* Crown Business, 2001.

Shermer, Michael. *The Believing Brain: From Ghosts and Gods to Politics and Conspiracies – How We Construct Beliefs and Reinforce Them as Truths.* Times Books, 2011. P. 5.

Silver, Nate. *The Signal and the Noise: Why So Many Predications Fail – But Some Don't.* Penguin, 2012.

Taleb, Nassim Nicholas. *AntiFragile: Things That Gain from Disorder.* Random House, 2012.

Taleb, Nassim Nicholas. *The Black Swan: The Impact of the Highly Improbable.* Random House, 2007.

Taleb, Nassim Nicholas. *Fooled by Randomness: The Hidden Role of Change in Life and in the Markets.* Random House, 2004.

Toynbee, Arnold. *Mankind and Mother Earth: A Narrative History of the World.* Oxford University Press, 1976.

Van Doren, Charles. *A History of Knowledge: Past, Present, and Future.* Ballentine, 1991.

West, Geoffrey. *Scale: The Universal Laws of Growth, Innovation, Sustainability, and the Pace of Life in Organisms, Cities, Economies, and Companies.* Penguin Press, 2017.

Wexler, Bruce. *Brain and Culture: Neurobiology, Ideology, and Social Change.* MIT Press, 2006.

PART 3: SKILL SHIFT

46 STRATEGY SHIFT: COMPLEXITY, ECOSYSTEM, SYSTEM DESIGN

Beer, Stafford. *Platform for Change.* Wiley, 1975.

Chandler, David G. *The Campaigns of Napoleon: The Mind and Method of History's Greatest Soldier.* MacMillan, 1966.

Diamond, Jared. *Guns, Germs, and Steel: The Fates of Human Societies.* Norton, 1999.

Forrester, Jay. Principles of Systems. Productivity Press, 1968, 1990.

Franklin, Daniel, Editor. *Megachange: The World in 2050.* Wiley, 2012.

Friedman, George. *The Next 100 Years: A forecast for the 21st Century.* Anchor Books, 2010.

Gore, Al. *The Future: Six Drivers of Global Change.* Random House, 2013.

Meadows, Donella, Dennis L. Meadows and Jorgen Randers. *Beyond the Limits: Confronting Global Collapse; Envisioning a Sustainable Future.* Chelsea Green, 1992.

Meadows, Donella H. and Diana Wright (Editor). *Thinking in Systems: A Primer.* Chelsea Green Publishing, 2008.

Miller, James Grier. *Living Systems.* McGraw Hill, 1978

Morris, Langdon. *Foresight and Extreme Creativity: Strategy for the 21st Century.* FutureLab, 2016.

Randers, Jorgen. *2052: A Global Forecast for the Next Forty Years.* Chelsea Green, 2012.

Rushkoff, Douglas. *Present Shock: When Everything Happens Now.* Current, 2014.

Smil, Vaclav. *Global Catastrophes and Trends: The Next Fifty Years.* The MIT Press, 2012.

Tainter, Joseph A. *The Collapse of Complex Societies.* Cambridge University Press, 1988.

The Economist. "Pulp Friction: Technology and International Trade." March 24, 2018, p. 69.

Toffler, Alvin. *Future Shock.* Random House, 1970.

50 LEADERSHIP SHIFT: ROLE, SURPRISE

Colvin, Geoff. *Talent Is Overrated: What Really Separates World-Class Performers from Everyone Else*. Portfolio, 2008.

Cronin, Vincent. *Napoleon*. HarperCollins, 1971.

Gerstner, Louis V. *Who Says Elephants Can't Dance?* HarperCollins, 2002.

Glassner, Barry. *The Culture of Fear: Why Americans Are Afraid of the Wrong Things*. Basic Books., 1999.

Handy, Charles. *The Age of Unreason*. Harvard Business Review Press, 1991.

Keegan, John. *Intelligence in War: Knowledge of the Enemy from Napoleon to Al-Qaeda*. Knopf, 2003.

Keegan, John. *The Mask of Command*. Penguin, 1987.

Pye, David. *The Nature and Art of Workmanship*. Cambridge University Press, 1968.

Watson, Peter. *The Modern Mind: An Intellectual History of the 20th Century*. HarperPerrennial, 2002.

53 ORGANIZATION SHIFT: WORK, AGILE, POWER, EXTREME, WORKSTYLE

Allen, Thomas J. and Gunter W. Henn. *The Organization and Architecture of Innovation*. Elsevier, 2007.

Bowman, Sharon L. *Training from the BACK of the Room: 65 Ways to Step Aside and Let Them Learn*. Pfeiffer, 2009.

Deming, W. Edwards. *The New Economics: Industry, Government, Education*. MIT Press, 2000.

Drucker, Peter. *Post-Capitalist Society*. HarperBusiness, 1994.

Litan, Robert E. *Trillion Dollar Economists: How Economists and Their Ideas Have Transformed Business*. Bloomberg Press, 2014.

Morris, Langdon. *Managing the Evolving Corporation*. Wiley, 1995.

Packard, David. *The HP Way*. HarperBusiness, 1995.

Ray, Paul H. and Sherry Ruth Anderson. *The Cultural Creatives: How 50 Million People Are Changing the World*. Three Rivers Press, 2000.

Reich, Robert B. *The Work of Nations*. Vintage, 1991, 1992.

Sabbagh, Karl. *Twenty-First Century Jet: The Making and Marketing of the Boeing 777*. Scribner, 1996.

Senge, Peter. *The Fifth Discipline: The Art & Practice of the Learning Organization*. Doubleday, 2006.

Shirky, Clay. *Here Comes Everybody: The Power of Organizing Without Organizations*. Penguin Books, 2008.

Wainwright, Tom. *Narco-nomics: How to Run a Drug Cartel*. Public Affairs Books, 2016.

59 INNOVATION SHIFT: INNOVATION PLANNING, TREND, 3D, SCENARIO PLANNING, BUSINESS MODEL, TECHNOLOGY ROADMAP, DESIGN THINKING, CREATIVE, CURIOSITY, FAILURE

Beckman, Sara L. and Michael Barry. "Innovation as a Learning Process: Embedding Design Thinking." *California Management Review*, Fall 2007.

Colvin, Geoff. *Talent is Overrated: What Really Separates World-Class Performance from Everybody Else*. Portfolio, 2008.

Conlon, Jerome, Moses Ma, and Langdon Morris. *Soulful Branding*. FutureLab Press, 2015.

Crawley, Edward, Bruce Cameron and Daniel Selva. *System Architecture: Strategy and Product Development for Complex Systems*. Pearson, 2016.

Csikszentmihalyi, Mihaly. *Creativity: Flow and the Psychology of Discovery and Invention*. Harper, 1996.

De Geus, Arie. *The Living Company*. Harvard Business Review Press, 1997.

Dorner, Dietrich. *The Logic of Failure: Recognizing and Avoiding Error in Complex Situations*. Perseus Books, 1986.

Eisner, Eliot. *The Arts and the Creation of Mind.* Yale University Press, 2002.

Judkins, Rod. *The Art of Creative Thinking.* Perigee, 2016.

Kahane, Adam. *Solving Tough Problems.* Berrett-Kohler, 1999.

Kahane, Adam. *Transformative Scenario Planning.* Berrett-Kohler, 2012.

Keeley, Larry. *The Ten Types of Innovation: The Discipline of Building Breakthroughs.* Wiley, 2013.

Kelly, Eamonn. *Powerful Times: Rising to the Challenge of Our Uncertain World.* Wharton School Publishing, 2006.

Long, David and Zane Scott. *A Primer for Model-Based System Engineering, 2nd Edition.* Vitech Corporation, 2011.

Mintzberg, Henry. *The Rise and Fall of Strategic Planning.* Free Press, 1994.

Moore, Geoffrey. *Crossing the Chasm.* HarperBusiness, 1991.

Mootee, Idris. *Design Thinking for Strategic Innovation.* Wiley, 2013.

Morris, Langdon, Moses Ma and Po Chi Wu. *Agile Innovation: The Revolutionary Approach to Accelerate Success, Inspire Engagement, and Ignite Creativity.* Wiley, 2014.

Morris, Langdon. *The Agile Innovation Master Plan.* Revised Edition. FutureLab, 2016.

Morris, Langdon. *The Innovation Formula: The Guidebook to Innovation for Small Business Leaders and Entrepreneurs.* Innovation Academy, 2015.

Osterwalder, Alexander and Yves Pigneur. *Business Model Generation.* Wiley, 2010.

Pijl, Patrick van der, Justin Lokitz and Lisa Kay Solomon. *Design a Better Business: New Tools, Skills, and Mindset for Strategy and Innovation.* Wiley, 2016

Ralston, Bill and Ian Wilson. *The Scenario Planning Handbook: Developing Strategies in Uncertain Times.* South-Western 206.

Rogers, Everett M. *Diffusion of Innovations.* Free Press, 1983.

Schoemaker, Paul J. H. *Profiting from Uncertainty: Strategies for Succeeding No Matter What the Future Brings.* Free Press, 2002.

Schwartz, Peter. *The Art of the Long View.* Doubleday Business, 1991.

Tharp, Twyla. *The Collaborative Habit: Life Lessons for Working Together.* Simon & Schuster, 2009.

Tharp, Twyla. *The Creative Habit: Learn It and Use It for Life.* Simon & Schuster, 2003.

PERIODICALS

The Economist, Foreign Affairs, The New York Review, and *Science* Magazine are very helpful resources for those interested in understanding the future and how it is emerging.

INDEX

33624744R00112

Printed in Great Britain
by Amazon